FACES OF PHILIP

ALSO BY JESSICA MITFORD

Daughters and Rebels

The American Way of Death

The Trial of Dr. Spock

Kind and Usual Punishment

A Fine Old Conflict

Poison Penmanship:
The Gentle Art of Muckraking

FACES OF PHILIP

A Memoir of Philip Toynbee

JESSICA MITFORD

ALFRED A. KNOPF   NEW YORK   1984

Library of Congress Cataloging in Publication Data

Mitford, Jessica.   Faces of Philip.

Includes index.
1. Toynbee, Philip—Biography. 2. Authors, English—20th century—
Biography. I. Title.
PR6039.08Z77   1984   823'.914.   84-47872
ISBN 0-394-53237-6

To: *Josephine*
    Polly
    Jason
    Lucy
    Clara

CONTENTS

Photo inserts follow pages 80 and 112

INTRODUCTION AND
ACKNOWLEDGEMENTS

When Philip Toynbee died in 1981, I had hoped that the many obituaries and articles about him, plus any letters that his widow Sally might value, could be preserved in a privately-printed pamphlet for his children and grandchildren. I broached this idea to his family and friends; all were for it in principle, but nobody actually took it on. So I began to think in terms of a memoir.

But what exactly *is* a memoir? I kept wondering as I got on with it. Something short of a biography, in which one must probe deeply into the subject's antecedents and childhood, the literary influences that shaped his writings, and record details of his comings and goings from cradle to grave.

Mine was a lot less ambitious, and I took comfort from the OED definition of memoir:

> A record of events, not purporting to be a complete history, but treating of such matters as come within the personal knowledge of the writer, or are obtained from certain particular sources of information.

In fact it was only after I had finished the book and begun to write this introduction that I thought to get Philip's entry in

Who's Who, which would have been the starting-point for a proper biography. I reproduce it here, in the minuscule print of that publication, for the benefit of some future biographer, or some yet-unborn PhD candidate who might wish to pursue the leads therein:

TOYNBEE, (Theodore) Philip; Novelist; foreign correspondent of The Observer and member of editorial staff since 1950; *b* 25 June 1916; *s* of late Arnold Joseph Toynbee, CH, FBA, and Rosalind, *d* of late Prof. Gilbert Murray, OM; *m* 1st, 1939, Anne Barbara Denise Powell (marr. diss. 1950); two *d*; 2nd, 1950, Frances Genevieve Smith; one *s* two *d*. *Educ:* Rugby Sch.; Christ Church, Oxford. Editor of the Birmingham Town Crier, 1938-39; commission in Intelligence Corps, 1940–42; Ministry of Economic Warfare, 1942–44; on staff of SHAEF in France and Belgium, 1944–45; Literary Editor of Contact Publications, 1945–46. *Publications:* The Savage Days, 1937; School in Private, 1941; The Barricades, 1943; Tea with Mrs Goodman, 1947; The Garden to the Sea, 1953; Friends Apart, 1954; Pantaloon, 1961; (with Arnold Toynbee) Comparing Notes: a Dialogue across a Generation, 1963; (with Maurice Richardson) Thanatos: A Modern Symposium, 1963; Two Brothers, 1964; A Learned City, 1966; Views from a Lake, 1968; Towards the Holy Spirit, 1973; (ed) The Distant Drum, 1976; contrib.: New Statesman and Nation, Horizon, New Writing, Les Temps Modernes. *Recreations:* gardening, bicycling. *Address:* Woodroyd Cottage, St Briavels, Lydney, Glos. *Club:* Oxford Union Society.
      See also Polly Toynbee.

Reading it over, I can see that large chunks of his life are missing from my book. Apart from the fact that I never knew his first name was Theodore and that his second wife whom we all know as Sally was christened Frances Genevieve, there was much else that I either was not aware of, or have forgotten. 'Editor of *Birmingham Town Crier*'? News to me, although I do remember visiting him in Birmingham in 1938, where he was working at some sort of journalistic job – but hadn't realized he was the editor. 'On staff of SHAEF'? Again, I knew he was in Belgium in the war, but hadn't known in what a grand capacity.

For my purpose, prime sources apart from my own memory were his books from which I have quoted, his diary and letters, and above all the recollections of his family and friends.

Like many another of his generation, Philip kept, with few lapses, a journal in which he recorded day by day every detail of his life. Sally kindly lent me some of the volumes, written in Philip's distinctive handwriting – not always totally legible, alas. The job of choosing bits to quote for the purpose of a short memoir was agonizing. Many an entry is a story in itself, a vignette of the period; while dashed off, as diaries are, they are bursting with Philip's singular character and style. One might hope that some day a publisher would see their value as a unique and idiosyncratic slice of the history of those years.

Pack rat that I am, I have kept Philip's correspondence with my husband Esmond Romilly for more than forty years. It turned up in a suitcase full of documents, old bank statements, expired passports and letters from my own family that I have lugged round during myriad moves. After Esmond's death in 1941, the Royal Canadian Airforce sent me a list of his belongings which, they said, they would send to me upon request. These included, '6 logs of wood, kindling wood and fire paper. 6 Woolworth Highball glasses. 1 Teapot . . . plus correspondence.' From America I wrote back declining the firewood and other assorted comforts of life, but asking for the letters, which eventually arrived; among them were several from Philip.

Sally produced letters from Elizabeth Bowen, Robert Nye and others. Ann Farrer sent her voluminous correspondence with Philip from 1977 to 1981. His daughter Polly had a small but useful stack of letters. Again – hard choices about what to quote; and the wish that some publisher might spring for a

collection of Philip's letters beginning with his first surviving effort, written when he was four:
'Dere Mummy and Daddy, I wrot this all by miself . . . '

Easily the most enjoyable part of preparing this book were the long talks with Philip's family and friends, and the correspondence that developed with some of them.

I went about this in what is perhaps a rather odd way, but it was the only method that worked for me. For the sake of accuracy I sent to each person interviewed my transcription of our conversation for corrections and/or emendations. Next, I flung around bits of draft in various stages to my interlocutors so that they could see how their words had been incorporated into the text – again, asking for their comments and any suggested changes.

While this worked well for corrections of fact – dates, places, identification of people – it also created problems. In *Julia*, Frances Partridge quotes Julia Strachey: 'I bethought me of the fact that virtually every story one hears related in an autobiography, biography or history has many different versions to it.' I bethought me of the same as I pondered over diverse – and divergent – accounts of Philip's separation from his first wife Anne. I finally decided it had become too complicated and murky, so I regretfully discarded them all in favour of Anne's one-liner: 'Just write, "The following year she left Philip and married Richard Wollheim." '

Another difficulty arose: what to do when, as sometimes happened, my correspondent took issue with my interpretation of events? For example both Sally and Philip's daughter Josephine thought that I had given a biased and too frivolous account of the Barn House Community (Chapter 10), so I asked them to write their own views of that strange episode. I have included their letters in full.

Thus my 'memoir' turns out to be the combined effort of a

number of people, rather than the work of one writer. My collaborators, to whom I am deeply grateful for the time and thought they put into helping to sort it all out, are identified and credited in the text.

There are two, however, to whom I owe a special debt: Ann Farrer (called Idden in family circles), my first cousin and best friend since childhood, who lives in Bucks; and the writer Patrick Leigh Fermor, who lives in Greece, whom I met only once, glancingly, years ago.

If ever the standard author's dedication '. . . without whom this book could not have been written' applied, it does to Ann and Paddy. Emboldened by their encouragement when I first bruited the idea of a memoir, I exploited them unmercifully, sending them chapters as I wrote for their advice and criticism.

These kind souls – and stout hearts – never failed me. They answered, usually by return of post, so that letters whizzed back and forth in triangular fashion between Bucks, Greece and California, where I live.

Reading over the corrected manuscript, I detect the results of their handiwork on almost every page, ranging from organization of subject matter to style, grammar, syntax.

To give but two examples from what Ann calls her 'mass of minutiae': she picked me up on Americanisms that she thought unsuited to an English readership – 'lavatory paper not toilet paper' – and on matters of taste. Robert Kee had told me an anecdote that I had used at the very end of the book, where Philip's friends sum up their feelings about him. '*Please* don't put that bear in there,' Ann wrote, and of course she was right; but as it is too good a bit of Toynbee lore to be missed, I give it here: Robert and Philip had gone to a party in the country. 'There was a huge stuffed bear with a slightly leering face, upright in the hall', Robert told me. 'Philip pointed to it and said "when I'm gone that's how I'd like to be – stuffed, with a pint of beer in my hand, stood up in a hall grinning at people." '

Paddy's first letter from Greece, a response to mine asking him for some memories of Philip in wartime and after, was a goldmine of material. But oh his handwriting! The Rosetta stone isn't in it. But like the decipherers of that stone I eventually caught on. My transliteration of Paddy's letter ran to nine single-spaced typed pages, his nuggets scattered throughout the book.

I sent him some chapters and soon had his answer, full of marvellously pungent, almost line-by-line, criticism and comments:

> 'Capitulated': Would something like 'gave in' be better? I'm all for dodging latinisms, if a respectable saxonism is handy. Otherwise the prose can go ballooning off in bubbles of Ciceronian rotundities, instead of being nailed down by short Saxon pegs.
>
> I have always hated 'explicate', though I know it's in common use. 'Develop'? or 'explain'? Explicate always makes me fidgety.

Another fidgety word was 'ongoing', deplored by Paddy: 'Not too keen on "ongoing". Isn't it what's called a "vogue word"? Perhaps "continuous", or "unfailing." '

In the same letter, the Paddy classic:

> Here's old 'Ongoing' again, and with a terrible though mercifully nonexistent yoke fellow, viz. 'comedic'. Comic's the word, and a jolly nice one too; tragedic to miss.
>
> I know 'scenario' is all the rage . . . couldn't it be 'a continuous', or 'serial', or 'never-ending' comedy? comic play?

Thanks to Paddy, the reader will search in vain for any explication, capitulation or ongoing comedic scenarios in these pages.

Lastly, I must thank some special friends in California – 'angelic encouragers', to quote a Philip expression – who helped in various ways: Bob Treuhaft, severe but indispensable critic; Gay Ducey, who kept track of the elusive files and gave much invaluable editorial advice; Marge Frantz, to whom a person like Philip was a total mystery and who kept me going by wanting to know more about him; Rita Wiggins, who kept our house afloat amidst a sea of old drafts, letters and other flotsam and jetsam; Marcie McGaugh and Maggie Rebhan, who did an expert job of typing the manuscript – in the course of which they got so interested in Philip's books that they ordered them through the University of California inter-library system.

FACES OF PHILIP

CHAPTER 1

Faces of Philip

In June 1980 I had a letter from Philip Toynbee saying:

> Believe it or not, I've just been asked to write your *Times* obituary. In some ways I see that this is tremendously one up on you – unless, of course, you've also been asked to write mine. *On the other hand*, it does give me a good deal of freedom, doesn't it: I mean either you'll never read it, or you'll read it From Beyond where all is fórgiven in every conceivable direction.

He added, 'All love – and please don't croak before I get this obit done. Drive carefully for next month or so.'

There followed a mock-acrimonious correspondence. I wrote back to say I found the whole idea preposterous as I knew he would send me up ('ha ha, in more ways than one') just when I was in no position to answer back. He responded, 'Would you send me a potted autobiography with dates of all books etc? Should you prefer it *write your own obit* – about six hundred words – and I promise (nearly) not to alter one of them.'

'Goodness you've got a nerve,' I answered.

> In other words – I should write the obit and you collect the fee
> whilst retaining what Film Folk call creative control over the
> content? NEVER. However I will send a list of my books in
> case the obit triggers a new demand for them, all a good thing
> for my Children's inheritance.

The list of books, their publishers and dates, followed with a
note to Philip:

> *Caution*: At least one of these is a false lead, slipped in to annoy
> and to test *yr* ability as researcher obit writer. Up to you to
> guess WHICH. This, needless to say, was Bob's* idea – he
> always thinks of my best jokes.

(The slipped-in false lead was *'Fair Game: Genuine Sportsmen's
Clubs or Cover for Vigilante Operation?* Weidenfeld, 1964' –
exactly the sort of boring cause/sociology book I might have
written, as Bob pointed out. But whether this made it into
Philip's six hundred words I shall, of course, never know.)

In the event, it was I who only a year later wrote an obituary
for Philip. He had been ill on and off for some months: colitis,
it was at first thought, though soon diagnosed as cancer;
however, the doctors believed that given a successful operation, he might live for years. After the surgery they pronounced his disease incurable – his death could be expected in a
matter of weeks or months. Wishing to say goodbye, I
arranged to go to see him as soon as he got out of hospital. The
telegram saying that he had died arrived the day before I was to
leave California.

I was pondering this appalling news in a fog of misery when
Terence Kilmartin rang up from London: *The Observer* was
compiling a page of reminiscences about Philip by various
friends, and wanted a thousand words from me. The deadline

* Bob Treuhaft, my husband.

was the next day, the copy to be telephoned in by 3 p.m. London time, 7 a.m. in California.

Fortified by strong coffee and stronger drink, I worked through the night searching for the elusive thousand words about my oldest friend. ('And what would HE like best?' I kept thinking.) I sifted through his letters, and found all sorts of possible false starts: one in which an Oxford don had described Philip as a 'washed-out Gary Cooper', to which I might comment that to me Gary C. was a washed-out Philip Toynbee? But no.

By early dawn in California I had finished. Philip's endearing capacity for self-mockery was the theme of my inadequate effort: 'Damn it, I'm supposed to be a cheery clown, not a melancholy brooder', he had written during one of the dreadful depressions that began to assail him some years before his death.

The memorial service, held on 17 July 1981, was preceded by a drink-up in El Vino, attended by Philip's two wives, his five children, Monmouthshire neighbours who had come up to London for the occasion, and a few London friends. The mood was convivial; oh how Philip would enjoy this reunion in his favourite Fleet Street haunt! I saw in my mind's eye his rugged, acne-scarred face with a lone tooth (the others having been knocked out in an altercation with a racialist bigot) peering down at us from the rafters.

The service itself, in the beautiful Church of St Bride in Fleet Street (where all good journalists are put to rest, I was told) was a fair disaster – but again, how Philip would have relished this aspect! Lessons were intoned, 'The Lord is my shepherd' was chanted, extracts from Philip's last book, *Part of a Journey*, were read out, Terry Kilmartin and Robert Kee spoke, the choir sang, the Blessing was pronounced by the Rector.

The entire performance was effectively drowned out by a high-pitched continuous whistle; we, the mourners, saw lips moving, expressions changing as speaker after speaker mounted the pulpit, but the audience heard not a word. Church officials – deacons? – were seen moving deftly and swiftly through the church with equipment – geiger counters? – trying to find the source of the noise: heating equipment out of order? A stuck organ stop? No: it proved to be a malfunctioning hearing aid of one of Philip's aunts. Another aunt, sitting next to her, was herself too deaf to notice. Oh Philip – *why* aren't you here (I thought) to savour this odd circumstance.

Years have now gone by, yet time and again some amusing incident will trigger the thought, 'I must write and tell Philip' – but there he isn't.

Philip, like most people, had a multi-sided personality. To me, he generally turned his clown's face. To my cousin Ann Farrer, who has generously sent me some of his letters, his compassionate critic's face. To the nuns whom he later came to love, his new-found religious face. To literary friends like Stephen Spender, Robert Nye and Patrick Leigh Fermor, his serious poet's face – behind which, however, there always lurked the twinkling grin.

I collected and read with enormous interest the obituaries that appeared in the London press. More and more I began to fathom the complexity of Philip's character, and to wish that the composite view of him that emerged from his friends' appraisals could be preserved in some permanent form.

How to get him into focus? Soon after his daughter Polly published her first book in 1964 at the age of seventeen, Philip said to me in his sly, wry way, 'These days I'm only known as the son of Arnold or the father of Polly.' That, of course, was an absurd if typical piece of self-deprecation; for thirty years, his weekly book reviews in *The Observer* were an outstanding feature, a treat to which innumerable fans turned first thing on Sunday morning.

Philip will doubtless be long remembered – and deeply missed – by thousands who knew him only through his reviews. Although he loved reviewing, and would have felt bereft without this work, he regarded it principally as a means of earning his daily bread. (I remember being shocked at the meagerness of the loaf. His wages at *The Observer* were a fraction of what top-flight American reviewers are paid by publications of like reputation and prestige.) But from boyhood on, as he saw it, his real vocation was that of novelist and poet, and not just *a* novelist – a *major* writer of experimental fiction.

At this point it would seem only fair to give Philip the floor to describe in his distinctive voice his own perceptions of his strivings, accomplishments and failures – after all, he had offered me this opportunity, had our roles been reversed.

In a rare autobiographical talk given at the Cheltenham Festival in 1976, the year he turned sixty, he promised the audience to be 'entirely frank', and to avoid both false modesty and false pride. 'Perhaps I should start by saying that I've always wanted to be a great writer and a good man; and that I've nearly always believed that the second is more important than the first.'

The book that he intended to be his 'first indubitable masterpiece' was *Tea with Mrs Goodman*, whose publication in 1947 far ante-dated the *Pantaloon* series, which he was still writing and re-writing almost to the end of his life. At that time he and his wife Anne were living on the Isle of Wight in

> a kind of paradise, a beautiful house between the downs and the sea. Unfortunately I was by no means ready for paradise, and kept roaring out of it and over the sea to London; crawling back again three or four days later with my tail between my legs,

leaving various disgraces behind me and slinking into my lair
like a wounded animal.

On his way back to the Isle of Wight by train and boat from
one of these disastrous excursions, he read a review of *Tea with
Mrs Goodman* in the *New Statesman* 'which praised the book to
the skies and ended by claiming – no less! – that English prose
would never be the same again.'

Philip read and re-read this golden tribute, 'sometimes
pausing to linger over some especially heady phrase – and by
the time the boat got to Ryde pier I must have read those two
columns at least fifty or sixty times.'

But after a day or two, 'spent as usual licking my London
wounds and slowly building up my strength to make another
confident assault on the capital', the magic faded, 'the words
became almost meaningless.' The master writer, the man who
had changed the whole direction of English prose, lay

> cowering in his bedroom, tormented by sleepless nights and
> the constant jabbing memories of recent humiliations . . . An
> utterly different Philip Toynbee: a weakling, an abysmal suf-
> ferer, a drunkard, and lecher, a self-obsessed neurotic.
>   Which was the *real* Philip Toynbee? Well, I suppose they
> were both real, in a sense [he told the Cheltenham audience].
> But how much more real, inevitably, the second seemed than
> the first!

He recalled Edmund Wilson's 'desperately truthful account of
the writer's condition – a giant on a typewriter, but to his wife
a pygmy and an invalid.' He did acknowledge a third role –
'the antique role of clown; and it was in this protective and
much appreciated part that I usually presented myself to my
friends.'

His goal, he wrote in his 1953 diary, was nothing less than to
write

that incontrovertible masterpiece which has drawn me forward for so long . . . All I know so far about my future book is
that it is to be a 'great' one – the *Faust, Iliad* or *Divine Comedy* of
our time . . . Here, then, I am to be the full representative of
my time, as Goethe was of his, and everything I have learned
and experienced will be made use of.

He once said to Robert Nye:

What I am trying to do in *Pantaloon* – no doubt over-
ambitiously – is to write something like a modern equivalent of
Don Quixote, The Prelude, Faust and *A la Recherche du Temps
Perdu*, all in one. That's to say a tragi-comic epic whose hero is
representative, but not in the least typical, of the years 1914–
50.

If this sounds like a parody of effusive schoolboy self-
puffery, it is in fact very far from that. It is middle-aged Philip
speaking quite seriously of his intentions, sustained over a
twenty-five-year period, to accomplish what he saw as an
important, and perhaps great, innovative and experimental
work of literature. 'I couldn't stop writing,' he wrote in his
diary, 'and I couldn't, without a great sense of futility, resign
myself to a lower ultimate ambition.'

Did he succeed in this portentous ambition, as he himself
described it? The verdict is not yet in, for the largest portion of
the *Pantaloon* series, some six volumes, still languishes in
manuscript. Multi-volume experimental novels in verse are
not, it seems, precisely what modern publishers are vying
for.

The four published volumes are *Pantaloon*, 1961; *Two
Brothers*, 1964; *A Learned City*, 1966; *Views from a Lake*, 1968.
These have a small but devoted readership of fellow-poets and
critics, some of whom discussed the series in their obituary
articles.

Patrick Leigh Fermor describes the

far-too-little-known, many volumed, and extremely brilliant narrative poem *Pantaloon*. Far more than a poetical feat of self-mockery, it is a most precious and perceptive documentation of a certain kind of growing-up, with all the problems, trends, dogmatic attractions and revolts to which the restless youth of the middle and late Thirties were prone.

To Stephen Spender, Philip was

an eccentric, almost Dostoevskian character who tried to live and write out of some demonic force of which he was conscious in himself as being his personal truth. His long semi-autobiographical poem, *Pantaloon* – the completed text of which has never been published – expresses this aim in literature . . . His verse epic – or at any rate passages of it – reflects his serious, religious, ribald, self-mocking attitude to life. His friends will remember him as a poignant and moving personality who lived his life almost as if he were the ironically self-viewing hero of a fiction written by himself.

Robert Nye, who corresponded with Philip for several years about *Pantaloon*, thought this work

a remarkable achievement, perhaps a masterpiece . . . It strikes me as one of the last authentic works of the spirit of modernism. Now Philip is dead it will no doubt be published and hailed as such. I hope he gets a laugh at the heavenly wicket.

In their obituary notices, Philip's friends almost unanimously paid tribute to the 'antique role of clown', wherein lay so much of his particular capacity to charm.

Noel Annan:

Two of Philip's most endearing qualities were his sense of gratitude and his sense of comedy. Just after the war people used to quote Edmund Wilson's image of the artist as Philoctetes, repelling and enraging the public with his suppurating

wound but killing falsity with his bow. Philip said: 'The great
thing about *The Observer* is that all you have to do is to show
your wound. They never ask to see your bow.'

Stephen Spender:

The last time I met him was at a special meeting of the
Bertorelli Luncheon club which, together with his friend Ben
Nicolson, he founded. He was wearing a false beard of Tol-
stoyan style, thus mocking the life of the writer on the commune.

Peter Vansittart:

He had elements of hunter, corsair, explorer, mystic, clown,
with ample room for eccentricity, false starts, mischief,
excruciating pleasure and dramatic melancholy . . . He would
enter Suffolk pubs with false beard and accent, undeterred by
the invariable 'Ah, Philip? What's it to be?' At his last appearance at Bertorelli's, he masqueraded as a veteran Russian
émigré.

These, then, are the views of what might now be known as
Philip's 'extended family', his London pals and literary co-
equals. They clearly loved his exuberant company, his sharp
humour, his sparkling conversation; and they benignly tolerated his frequent falls from metaphorical grace, which of a late,
drunken evening too often took the form of corporeal prat-
falls.

What about his actual family? – or rather, families, for there
were two: Anne Powell, to whom he was married from 1939
to 1949, their daughters Josephine and Polly; and Sally Smith,
whom he married in 1950 and their three children Jason, Lucy
and Clara.

For these, life with Philip as they described it to me
must have been something of a roller-coaster ride: joyous,

exhilarating ups followed by agonizing, thudding downs.

For me, he was the one remaining link with the vanished pre-World War II life when for a year or so, as Esmond Romilly's best friend, he was a constant companion and perpetual source of enjoyment. Our friendship survived a lapse of sixteen years. When I saw him again in 1955, and thereafter quite often, he seemed fairly unchanged – as comical and fascinating as ever. Had he 'matured', to use a current vogue word for grown up? Not appreciably, thank goodness. In fact his youthful qualities – his propensity for wild enthusiasms, often dropped as hastily as they had been adopted; his restless search for answers to imponderable questions – had, if anything, become more pronounced than ever in middle age.

It was Philip's book *Friends Apart*, a memoir of Esmond Romilly and Jasper Ridley, both killed in the war, that gave me the idea of writing my own book about Esmond and me, eventually published under the title *Hons and Rebels*. I shall never forget bringing him the manuscript – in great trepidation, for this was my first effort at writing – and his daunting first words: 'What *extraordinary* paper.' (It was an American brand called 'corrasable bond', unknown in England.)

He was extremely nice about the book, and gave it its first boost: 'Wonderfully funny, very poignant,' he wrote to the publisher, words which when seen by me on the book jacket caused supreme delight. But as he read through the manuscript he kept saying 'Not nearly enough about ME.'

Thereafter I sent him drafts of all my subsequent books – on funerals, the trial of Dr Spock, American prisons, the muckraking collection. While he lavished undeserved praise (and equally undeserved opprobrium: 'I thought your spurious research came off rather well . . .') he always had a footnote: 'Nothing about ME?'

So here goes, Philip – '*All* about ME,' as I can hear you saying From Beyond, where all is forgiven in every conceivable direction.

CHAPTER 2

Rotherhithe Street

' "I really don't belong to these people, nice though many of them are. I don't quite belong to any people except to Esmond and Decca." ' I was amazed – not to say deeply touched – to read in *Friends Apart* this quotation from Philip's 1938 diary. However, he added: 'This was a miscalculation, as I gradually discovered when I was living with them, but the occasional spectacle of their loving and lawless life had made me believe that it was exactly the life for me.'

When my copy of *Friends Apart* arrived in California, I had not seen Philip for fifteen years, having left England in 1939. We had long stopped corresponding, and he had pretty much receded to the back of my mind, as people do after long absence. He inscribed the book 'To Decca with love, happy memories, and, please, no offence.' There was indeed no offence – on the contrary; and happy memories flooded back.

His book, as described in the introduction, is 'a fragmentary autobiography as well as a double memoir.' As this implies, it tells as much about Philip as it does about his two subjects. Apparently Esmond and Jasper represented to Philip opposite attractive poles, exemplifying what he perceived as a dichotomy that in various guises persisted to the end of his life. These two had never met each other, hence were conveniently pigeon-holed for their biographer.

Jasper, one gathers, personified the pleasurable sybaritic world of intellect, culture, elegance; Esmond, the earthier world of politics and action. To my mind Jasper remains in this book an elusive, rather shadowy character, his charm for Philip stated but never really explained. Esmond, on the other hand, comes straight to life, first as a farouche schoolboy rebel, later as a purposeful anti-fascist warrior in Spain, and finally as a volunteer airforce navigator in World War II.

Their friendship began early in 1934 when Philip, then 17, ran away from Rugby, his goal to join 15-year-old Esmond, a recent fugitive from Wellington, already a lodestar for runaway schoolboys. Esmond had established headquarters in the Parton Street Bookshop, a left-wing hangout from which he published and edited *Out of Bounds*, a magazine whose improbable objective was to foment revolution in England's public schools. Its masthead proclaimed its editorial policy: '*Out of Bounds* will openly champion the forces of progress against the forces of reaction on every front, from compulsory military training to propagandist teachings.'

Esmond and his publication had been the subject of many a lurid newspaper account: RED MENACE IN PUBLIC SCHOOLS!; OFFICER'S SON SPONSORS EXTREMIST JOURNAL; WINSTON CHURCHILL'S RED NEPHEW RUNS AWAY FROM SCHOOL: 'UNDER INFLUENCE OF LONDON COMMUNISTS,' SAYS MOTHER . . .

This was exactly what Philip, straining restively against the infuriating restrictions of Rugby, had been looking for: 'I began to pretend that I, too, like the bold Wellington boy, would run away from school and become a rebel in London.'

Soon the pretence became an obsession. Philip, having left a valedictory note for his headmaster, caught a train to London and found his way (by taxi, no less!) to Parton Street: 'That shop! the archetype of all the "People's Books", "Workers'

Bookshops", "Popular Books" that I was to know so intimately in the next five years.'

There follows a classic description of Esmond:

> A boy was leaving the shop as my taxi drew up in Parton Street, a short, square, dirty figure with a square white face and sweaty hair. 'I'm looking for Esmond Romilly,' I said.
> 'Yes?'
> He was instantly, dramatically, on his guard, conspiratorial, prepared for violent aggression or ingenious deceit. I thrilled and trembled more hysterically than ever.
> 'I'm Toynbee,' I said. 'Toynbee of Rugby.'
> Esmond looked sharply up and down the short street, then opened the shop door and pushed me through.

Philip explained that he had run away. 'He was instantly enthusiastic. "You can sleep on a mattress," he said, "and you can be joint editor. As for money, I get along all right with occasional journalism. You ought to manage . . ." '

In the next few days Philip, mesmerized, worked with Esmond interviewing *Out of Bounds* correspondents from other public schools; together they joined in the anti-fascist protest against Sir Oswald Mosley's monster meeting at Olympia where they were beaten and bloodied by blackshirt thugs. These were euphoric experiences. But in the rare moments when Philip was alone, he was assailed with terror and shame for the

> enormity, the irrevocability of my offence. Oh, God, why had I done it, why had I ruined my life, branded myself forever as the black sheep who had run away from school! . . . Did I even wish to escape? I was no Esmond Romilly, to keep my head indefinitely above the phosphorescent waters.

The Parton Street interlude came to an abrupt end when, to Esmond's furious disapprobation, Philip caved in to family pressure and a letter from his Rugby housemaster:

'If they've traced you here,' said Esmond, who had read the
letter over my shoulder, 'you'll have to move. I know a place
you could go.'
   'I'm going back,' I said. 'I must telegraph at once.' And in
my panic to submit, I was impervious even to his snarled and
outraged contempt. I packed my suitcase and hurried away
from the terrible little shop, from the terrible square figure at
the door.

Expelled – albeit gracefully and painlessly – from Rugby,
Philip agreed to his mother's proposal that he should spend six
months in a monastery cramming for an Oxford scholarship.
'Meanwhile I was neither to see nor to communicate with
Esmond Romilly, for my parents had quickly and easily
guessed his great influence over me and the alarmed admiration which I felt for him.'
   In spite of roadblocks thrown up by parents, schoolmasters
and his own mixed feelings, Philip's friendship with Esmond
grew and eventually flourished – a green bay tree, perhaps,
from the point of view of the elders, but durable to the end.
   In the summer of 1936 Esmond, telling friends that he was
going on a bicycle tour of France, headed for Spain and
enlisted in the International Brigade – at eighteen, he was the
youngest volunteer in that dedicated band. Over Christmas of
that year Philip led an international student delegation on a
tour of Spanish Republican strongholds: 'I felt so wildly
excited and yet so wretched at being a "student delegate",'
he wrote. In Spain he learned from General Kléber, commander of the International Brigade, of the disastrous battle
of Boadilla in which most of the English volunteers had
perished; but Kléber said he believed that Esmond was alive.
In fact he was one of only two survivors of the English group.
Suffering from dysentery, he was sent home on sick leave, and
was assigned the harrowing task of visiting the families of his
fallen English comrades to give them a first-hand account of
the battle.

Shortly after the New Year, Philip and Esmond met in
London. Philip detected a perceptible change in his friend: 'I
felt that rare disquiet which is caused by a surprising and as yet
unsounded alteration in someone we know well . . . He was
serious, quiet and reasonable; he was not in the least embit-
tered.' Philip's diary entry of that day describes their meeting:

(Jan 11, 1937):

    . . . after lounging about for an hour or so I called on Esmond.
    Nobody was at home but soon Mrs R. came in. She was her
usual self and for two hours, nearly, I sat deferentially listening
to the glories that are Giles* and Esmond.
    For all her obvious lack of feeling I couldn't help being sorry
for her. She valued Giles very highly. Esmond had gone to
Southampton to visit the mother of one of the Englishmen
who was killed beside him.
    He came in, very abrupt and yet polite. He was glad to see
me, and I felt an almost overwhelming affection for him. He's
changed – he looked well tho he told me he'd got dysentery!
He's quite changed.
    There's less bombast, far more maturity and a sort of odd
gentleness which was seldom apparent before.
    He ate ravenously and presently Mrs R. went out and left us.
Then he started to unburden himself, glad that with me he
needn't keep up the 'heroic fighters for freedom' talk. He told
me of awful disorganization in the International Column, of
disgruntlement, harsh criticism of each other, disgraceful re-
treats, cold, uncongenial company, military discipline and the
rapid fading of romance. He was miserable that Giles had gone
– said he knew G. wouldn't be able to stand it. He told me of
the terror of being machine-gunned from the air, and how the
bombs and shells sickened one with long accumulated fear. He
said the Spanish C.P. did everything and the 5th Regiment had
saved Madrid.
    I asked him whether he was a Communist and he said he was
afraid he'd have to say 'yes.' 'Why afraid?' and he explained
that the drilling and discipline and organizing of the Party was

---

* Giles Romilly, Esmond's older brother.

necessary, but wd squeeze all the beauty out of the Spanish nature. I saw what he meant.

R. had asked him to make recruiting speeches and he'd refused. I like him for that. He'd refused because he wouldn't deceive people about the misery and lack of glory. He told me about Boadilla where Arnold Jeans and other Englishmen in the Thaelmann Battalion were killed. Eighty of them isolated by a sudden retreat of the French on their right. Six hours and only 14 left alive!*

Esmond is a genuinely feeling person beneath all his toughness. I was amazed how little he dramatized, and he made me feel the tragedy of this war as never before. Every day of it is a tragedy because every day is a day of militarization, standardization . . .

Esmond will go back as soon as his illness is cured, and hopes to find Giles and Tony† at Albacete. I loved him and longed to implore him not to go back. At first I was self-conscious, rather on the defensive, expecting him to be contemptuous of me for not fighting. He so clearly wasn't – has so clearly learned to be tolerant and understanding.

His tolerance is a new thing – but he described how Scott Watson had ratted and the comrades had been harsh and bitter, and how he felt it was pure luck, 'courage' or the lack of it. And I agree with every word.

A few weeks later, in March 1937, Esmond and I made our own successful getaway to Spain.‡ Although we were second cousins, and almost of an age (he was eighteen and I nineteen) we had never met, until as Philip put it 'by the kind of improbable coincidence which we now suspect to be unconsciously contrived by those who are involved in it', I was invited for a weekend by an elderly relation, Cousin Dorothy Allhusen. Cousin Dorothy was one of the very few grown-ups that Esmond tolerated – in fact, actually liked. I arrived to

* Twelve Germans, two English.
† Tony Heineman.
‡ Described in *Hons and Rebels*, published in the United States as *Daughters and Rebels*.

find that he was staying there, recuperating from his dysentery.

In Philip's view, I was

> a girl who seemed to have been specially constructed to suit Esmond as a wife. Decca Mitford was the younger sister of two formidable women who, at this time, were shocking and entertaining the newspaper public by their fascist views and behaviour. She herself had already declared herself a political extremist, though her extremism was in the opposite direction from her sisters'.

The 'formidable' sisters were Diana, who subsequently married Sir Oswald Mosley, and Unity, who spent most of her time in Germany as part of Hitler's inner circle. My parents had also become devotees of the Nazi creed. Being in full opposition to all they stood for – and having declared myself 'a Communist' – I had long sought an escape route from this incompatible milieu; and, like Philip, had read a lot about Esmond and admired him and his politics from afar. His book, *Out of Bounds: The Education of Giles and Esmond Romilly*, written in collaboration with his brother and published in 1935, had become my beacon.

Ten days after meeting Esmond I fled with him to Bilbao, pursued by British consuls and other unpleasant types including Anthony Eden (then Foreign Secretary), who at my parents' instigation sent a destroyer to fetch us back to England. My father had contrived to make me a Ward in Chancery, subject to being put in a Home for Wayward Girls unless I obeyed the Chancery judge's instructions. It was all to no avail. Esmond pointed out to the commander of the destroyer that he had no legal right to hold us; penalties for forcible abduction could be severe. This argument proved to be persuasive, and we were put ashore in France. We settled in Bayonne where after a good bit of turbulence, as airline pilots put it, we were married in June 1937.

Philip 'greedily followed' these events from the newspaper accounts and was delighted to read that banns had been put up in the British Consulate in Bayonne: 'Within a week we read in the *Daily Express*: NO KISSES AS JESSICA IS MARRIED.'

> Nineteen-year-old Mrs Esmond Romilly – Miss Jessica Freeman-Mitford, daughter of Lord Redesdale – rushed excitedly from a room in the British Consulate here today. Then she went off with her husband. They had been married ten minutes . . .

And he adds, 'Mrs Romilly and Lady Redesdale had been present at the wedding, and Esmond had secured the respectability which had become, by its denial to him, for once desirable.'

By the time I first met Philip, in the autumn of 1937, the events of 1934 which had led to his friendship with Esmond were ancient history – or what at that age seemed to pass for such. Philip was now at Christ Church, the first (and doubtless last) Communist to be elected President of the Oxford Union. Esmond and I were working for an advertising agency, he as copywriter at a wage of £5 a week, I as a market researcher for £2.10s. Philip describes his first visit to our house in Rotherhithe Street:

> I took a tram for miles along the Jamaica Road from the Elephant and Castle, and then I was lost for twenty minutes among the dark wharves and warehouses of Rotherhithe. When I asked a muffled stranger the way, he said: 'What ship do you want, mate?' and I knew that I was in authentic Esmond territory.

41 Rotherhithe Street, in the Bermondsey district, 'wasn't' (Philip wrote) 'a house like anybody else's; it was a thin little slice of a building, sandwiched between the warehouses which line the south bank of the river.' We shared it with Roger Roughton, a Communist poet who was a friend of Esmond's.

The rent, even for those days and that neighbourhood, was wonderfully cheap: four storeys, fully furnished, at £2 a month, of which we paid half.

I thought it was a lovely house, and perfect for the sharing arrangement. The ground floor consisted of a dining room and kitchen. The first floor was the drawing-room, complete with a grand piano – sadly out of tune, but often in use for parties. The two upper floors, of which Esmond and I occupied the top one, were divided into small bedrooms, allowing plenty of space for visitors to stay. (Much later, in the 1950s, some of the seven Rotherhithe Street houses in our row were smartened up, the impetus supplied by Antony Armstrong-Jones when he took one of them and, according to the newspapers, transformed it from a slum dwelling into a well-appointed love nest for Princess Margaret, whom he was then courting. *The Observer* (14 May 1961), describing the houses as 'old but not beautiful – rather ramshackle', reported that John Betjeman and other conservationists had made unsuccessful efforts to save them from the wrecker's ball and noted in passing, 'Literature, too, has found inspiration hereabouts. In one of these houses Jessica Mitford and Esmond Romilly, the Hon. and the Rebel, lived together before the war.' How amused we would have been, in 1937, had anyone then foretold that decades later our brief tenancy in Rotherhithe Street would be deemed to confer something approaching Historical Landmark status on our dilapidated dwelling!)

As for my own first impressions of Philip – it took me a while to single him out from what he describes in *Friends Apart* as Esmond's 'classless riff-raff of friends'. They were all new, and fascinating, to me, cut off as I was by choice and circumstance from most of my previous acquaintances. (Efforts of the latter to renew friendship of deb dance days were on the whole singularly unsuccessful. A former fellow-deb came to tea one day. 'I was terrified of coming down to the slums so I wore my oldest clothes,' she said; to which I replied crossly, 'You needn't have bothered, as your best clothes look like most people's oldest.' She never came back.)

In Philip, I noted early on, were combined all my favourite characteristics: he was a gifted and very funny raconteur, and a perfect target for teasing, one who readily joined in the laughter against himself. But there was also his serious dedication to the causes that Esmond and I held paramount: antifascism, and the eventual triumph of socialism.

His amazingly versatile love life, and the high drama with which he invested his accounts of its fluctuations, were an unfailing source of wonder and amusement; as good as going to the theatre, Esmond said, whenever he came round to chat. Esmond was constantly demanding the next act: 'We've paid our money and we expect a full evening's entertainment.' Philip seldom disappointed, and we must have been a good audience: 'Both of them listened with that greedy smacking of lips which I found so rewarding,' he wrote. 'It was one of Esmond's most charming characteristics that he could listen with almost inexhaustible pleasure to other people's stories.'

I remember those stories – and us, Oliver Twists, asking for more, or sometimes a repeat of one that we had heard many times. A particularly successful comic act was Philip's imitation of his mother, in the days when she was bending every effort to detach him from Esmond's noxious company. She had once said, 'To you, Esmond represents rotten meat.' Although I never met Philip's mum, her tones of outrage as rendered by him conjured her up most convincingly – Esmond doted on this putrefactive characterization and would always announce himself to Philip on the telephone as 'Your rotten meat merchant. I've an interesting consignment of old lights and livers for you, Mr Toynbee.'

How he loved – longed for love – suffered for love! Sometimes he came to stay with us for days at a time enabling us, voyeurish spectators at the dress-rehearsal, to observe the development of the drama-in-progress. The *mise-en-scène* would typically be one of our frequent bottle parties, the only sort of social gathering that anyone in our crowd could afford; guests were expected to bring drinks of their choice to be consumed on the premises, or with luck only partially consumed, leaving a little something to last the hosts through the coming week.

On these occasions Philip would get outrageously drunk. He would fling himself about muttering '*God* I want to sleep with somebody!' and would proposition any unattached girl in sight: 'Could you possibly stay on after the party and go to bed with me?' To my amazement, this indiscriminate approach sometimes worked, and Esmond and I would get up in the morning to find that there was one more for breakfast.

What was the secret of his success? As in any human endeavour, dogged, single-minded perseverance was doubtless a large part of it, for Philip hardly resembled the Young Lothario of the average maiden's dreams. He was large, rangy, and despite his considerable prowess as an athlete – as a schoolboy, he had been a rugby football star – uncoordinated as a wolfhound puppy. He was plagued by outbreaks of late-blooming acne, and his clothing was unkempt in the extreme.

Patrick Leigh Fermor, who first knew Philip a few years later, thought his appearance extraordinary:

> He looked like a huge, raw-boned aristocratic lumber-jack or stevedore. His clothes were unbelievably raffish and baggy, looking as if they had been slept in – which they often had: frayed tweed jacket with holes or old leather patches at the elbows, a check flannel shirt, a stringy and moulting tie, and foot-gear as clumping as army issue. He looked a bit grey and lantern-jawed on bad mornings; his brows were often furrowed, his complexion cratered here and there like a planet; and yet it was a strong distinguished face, however battered, with decisive features and a high and thoughtful brow. It was

often divided by a slit of a grin made very comic and dissolute by an isolated fang on one side, rather like Disney's Pluto; all its neighbours were absent through some mishap. He had a deeply-pitched attractive voice, sometimes with a hoarse rasp to it, and he spoke fluently and well, often very urgently, about history, politics and people.

His laugh was like the hiss of a soda-syphon. He could be very funny and he had an excellent ear for intonations; and he always emerged from his stories in a comic and clown-like role. I don't think he had any vanity at all. There was nothing affected about his untidy appearance, no note of feigned proletarianism, although I think he rather enjoyed his fortuitous rough-diamond air.

The aphrodisiac, then, must have been compounded of his intelligence, his marvellous jokes, above all his restless, often undirected energy. As Paddy said:

> In spite of his wild and battered appearance and frequent poor shape, I don't think girls were a difficult problem. For those who weren't alarmed, there was something unusual, arresting, which shone through the wolf's clothing and turned initial recoil into sympathy and attraction.

Besides Philip's love affairs (not all of which were trivial – some required much thought and discussion), what did we talk about? Esmond's work, Philip's writing, and, of course, politics.

Esmond's principal account at the advertising agency was Bob Martin's Dog-Plus Condition Powders, for which he had to prepare a weekly radio commercial, to be broadcast by Radio Luxembourg. The framework he had devised was a conversation between two dogs. He and Philip spent hours developing and refining these mini-dramas. They would assume various canine roles whilst I made notes, to be transcribed later for the radio script. Sometimes they staged routine dogfights in which the lucky dog whose owner fed him Bob

Martin's Powders would of course prevail; sometimes a sort of subliminal class-consciousness found its way into the script. Thus Esmond, a scruffy little mongrel on the prowl, would come sniffing up to Philip, a prancing thoroughbred being led through Hyde Park by his master's footman. 'Grrr – grrr,' mongrel Esmond would bark. 'Ullo, mate, you seem a bit down in the mouth today or should I say down in the jowl, ha ha, yap-yap-yap.' Thoroughbred Philip, infuriated by the gratuitous insult from an evident inferior, would reply in the snootiest of upperclass accents and strain to slip his leash; to no avail, for his miserly rich owner had neglected to furnish Bob Martin's Powders.

Philip would often appear with chunks of his inevitable book-in-progress:

> Sometimes I read passages of my new book to the Romillys. (Later Jasper's unspoken disrespect and the hostility of my party persuaded me to put it aside.) Esmond enjoyed, I think, all that was worst in this very bad book, and objected only to those emotional passages which gave it a rare flicker of reality. 'Too intense!' he would say, whenever I suggested that my hero was distressed; for he had no patience with any form of suffering which hadn't the excuse of poverty or bereavement. When he read books he liked them to be robust, zestful and as full as possible of eating, drinking, and making love. It was not surprising that when he came back from America in 1941 he had become a relentlessly insistent admirer of Thomas Wolfe.

Philip's diary entries for those years are a dizzying *mélange* of Communist Party activities interspersed with deb dances, drunken episodes, and night-long discussions with fellow Oxford intellectuals – Isaiah Berlin, Frank Pakenham, Maurice Bowra, Roy Harrod. Leafing through the diary, one wonders how he ever had time to study; but he must have found the odd moment, for he ended his Oxford career with a quite respectable Second in history.

July 20, 1936. to King Street [Communist Party headquarters] to buy a Daily (I feel oddly more devoted to it after Oxford and campaigning) . . . lunch with Esmond . . . A hot bath and then a last minute panic about buttons for my white waistcoat which ended in E. ringing up Moira and me just managing with some of Giles's. (E. has never worn a stiff shirt. He was rather contemptuous of me but extremely benevolent.) I took a taxi to Moira's and found Christian [Howard] and Juliet [Henley] dining – I, ¼ hour late! I fell easily, and quite gracefully into my "society bolshy" role, but at port with – I quite impressed him by telling him how much I loved my country and therefore had to be a Com.

Nov. 7, 1937 . . . I behaved abominably of course, being rather drunk. I kissed J. passionately outside . . . full of shame to bed. And so I should be! This awful behaviour must stop for good and all.

Denis Winnard, a fellow-student radical, described the Philip of that time as a bit of a trial to his long-suffering co-workers in a letter to me of September 1983:

My general feeling was that while intellectually and emotionally attracted by revolutionary politics (and he was one of the few open Communists) Philip was unable or unwilling to forgo the personal and social pleasures open to him. So it was difficult not to have reservations about his total reliability. This resulted (if my memory serves me) in his being excluded, at least in the period of my own involvement, from the inner circle of the student Communist Party.

Philip was forever trying to recruit us into the Party. Had he but known (and perhaps he did, in a way), he was a major deterrent to our joining at that time. We were, in principle and practice, in total sympathy with the CP's programme – devoted fellow travellers; but Philip's accounts of the Party's internal bickering and rigid sectarianism, which he couldn't resist telling in the most amusing fashion in the midst of his recruiting pitches, were hardly persuasive.

The ceaseless conflict that kept him shuttling between the rugged life of class struggle and the seductive, readily available delights of upper-class living made for excellent entertainment. For example, the Party assigned him to a fortnight's organizing job in which he was to stay in the cottage of an unemployed miner. At the bottom of his suitcase lay full-fig white tie and tails, in anticipation of a forthcoming weekend at Castle Howard (that amazing pile, seen on television by millions in *Brideshead Revisited*, where Philip had spent much of his childhood). His simulated fear, should the miner chance to look under the bed and into the suitcase, was one of his better comic turns, and the 'recruiting session' would soon dissolve into laughter.

Esmond and I joined the Labour Party's Bermondsey branch, which was so far to the left of the Party leadership as to be almost indistinguishable from the CP in its programme and activities. We immersed ourselves in the day-to-day drudgery of neighbourhood political work, which seemed to us more real – and far more productive – than Philip's exotic Oxford CP efforts.

Come May Day we would all march together, Communists and Labour members, for many miles to the gigantic rally in Hyde Park. Philip taught us all the Communist songs, Communist parodies of traditional songs and parodies of these parodies. If I shut my eyes, I can see the three of us sitting in the Rotherhithe Street drawing-room, or striding arm-in-arm in the May Day parade, lustily singing forth. Amongst the songs I still remember, my favourites were:

Class conscious we are
And class conscious we'll be,
And we'll TREAD ON THE NECK of the Bourgeoisie.

(According to Philip, the children of Communists who learned this ditty thought that the Bourgeoisie was a sort of huge snake.)

He had composed a tease on the Labour Party's official anthem the Red Flag, which starts: 'The people's flag/Is deepest red;/It shroudeth oft our martyred dead.' Philip's version went: 'The people's flag/Is palest pink;/It's not as red as you might think.'

There was a glorious free-form mixture of two versions of 'La Carmagnole', and 'Ça Ira', and yet a third I can't place, which went something like this:

> M'sieur Laval avait promis, M'sieur Laval avait promis
> De faire baisser le prix de la vie, de faire baisser le
>   prix de la vie.
> La vie c'est renchérie, Laval est dégonflé
> Tout Paris en rigole – vive le son du canon!
>
> Ça ira, ça ira, ça ira – tous les fascistes à la lanterne.
> On les pendra
> Et – si on ne les pend pas, on leur cassera la gueule.
> Si on ne les pend pas, la gueule on leur cassera.*

Best of all was an American song, rendered by Philip in what he conceived as an American Jewish immigrant's accent:

> Oh the cloak maker's union is a no-good union,
> It's a company union by the boss.
> Oh, the right-wing cloakmakers and the socialist fakers
> Are making by the workers double-cross.

The chorus – sung with feeling in Philip's vehement, rather hoarse, yet tuneful voice:

* Monsieur Laval had promised
   To lower the cost of living.
   The cost of living has risen, Laval is deflated
   All Paris is laughing at him – long live the sound
     of cannon!
   Everything's fine – string up all the Fascists.
   And if we don't hang them we'll smash in their faces.

Oh the Greens, the Hillquits and the Thomases,
They make by the workers false promises.
They preach socialism but they practice fascism
To preserve capitalism by the boss.

Years later, I was to hear this song sung in American left-wing gatherings. My newfound colleagues were quite surprised to find that I, a foreigner, knew all the lyrics.

Philip's own favourite of these myriad jingles may have more accurately summarized his own assessment of his CP experience:

> I had joined the University Communist Party at the end of my first term [he writes in *Friends Apart*], and month by month from December 1935 onwards I retired further and further into this busy and secretive hive. There was a song which we would ruefully sing at our evening socials:
>
>> Dan, Dan, Dan!
>> The Communist Party man,
>> Working underground all day.
>> In and out of meetings
>> Bringing fraternal greetings,
>> Never sees the light of day.

He never divulged to us his growing restiveness with the party of his choice, but his diary entry of 17 February 1937, written almost a year before his efforts to recruit Esmond and me, records his frustration:

> I wonder sometimes – and tonight is one of them – how I ever got myself into this ludicrously unsuitable position. I joined the Party 16 months ago: it was to be a spare time activity! Now it has eaten me all up. Takes every bit of me and pushes me into a mould which is uncomfortable and unsound. Artificial application of dogma won't do! I'm unhappy and I believe I could do better work in other ways – not so useful perhaps but *better*. Christ, I *must* get out of this racket or I'll go mad! . . . Oh! I *won't* be warped this way; I *will* read and write

and drink and kiss and lie in the sun. I haven't a shadow of conscience – only a fear of overwhelming opposition from stupid people . . . If only I could be among sharp, harsh clever people – or kind wise people. But the FOOLS are not my cup of tea.

Some forty years later, in his speech at the 1976 Cheltenham Festival, Philip reflected on another aspect of his membership in the Communist Party: his lifelong effort (as it turned out) to be a good man. Esmond and I were perhaps too insensitive, or too self-preoccupied, to discern this as a serious and enduring side of Philip's character; in any event, being good was never conspicuously on our own agenda. If he harboured such thoughts at the time, he did not communicate them to us, presumably for fear of our derision. But I suspect that what he told the Cheltenham audience was mostly hindsight:

> As for being a good man it was, of course, a long time before I began to think about the connection between that and writing . . . For me, during the three active years of my Party membership, being a good man was simply equated with being a good member of the Communist Party. True, it was in many ways a rather moralizing and puritanical party: I was often in trouble with my working-class bosses for getting drunk too often, or at least too flamboyantly, and for trying too hard to get myself as many girls as possible . . .
>
> To be a good Communist – dutiful, enthusiastic, hard-working, loyal and obedient – was to be a good man. And those outside the party were judged by the same fundamental standard: to what extent were they serving or hindering the revolutionary cause?

To 'drink and kiss and lie in the sun' was all very well, yet despite his reckless promiscuity Philip deeply longed for the stability of marriage. Esmond and I were unaware of this unusual yearning – a side of his character, like his desire to be a good man, that he would have concealed from us – but his

diary entries make it clear. Today, these may seem charmingly
old-fashioned, almost Jane Austenish, for marriage was
always on his mind.

For some months, a year or so before I met him, Philip was
courting Juliet Henley. He asked her to come to Oxford:

> Juliet wrote a sweet letter saying she was too broke to come –
> so I've sent her £1. How I hope she will! I still think that
> nothing could be nicer than to marry her . . . but alas! it is most
> unlikely.

Juliet is my second cousin. We are related through the
redoubtable and eccentric Stanleys of Alderley, our common
ancestry shared by such disparate characters as Bertrand
Russell, Algernon Swinburne, Esmond Romilly and count-
less others, including somewhere along the line Philip himself.
We were an inbred lot.

To our uncles and aunts, it was received wisdom that 'bad
Stanley blood' accounted for the unfortunate way the Mitford
girls turned out. It was a view from which Philip appears to
have derived some comfort, for I find recorded in his diary a
conversation in which I had told him that Juliet thought him
attractive; 'And then I thought of something else that Decca
said: "Those Stanleys know their own minds!" I repeated this
to myself a lot.'

Juliet remembers meeting Philip

> in all sorts of places ranging from Lyons Corner House at
> Marble Arch to Castle Howard. Oh, what a stimulating
> companion he was, by any standards, but most especially by
> contrast with those smooth, soppy drips who haunted the
> London ballroom scene. He was bursting with vitality,
> energetic, provocative, even sometimes outrageous. I wonder
> now if there was a deep strain of melancholy underlying so
> much ebullience?

Philip laced his courtship with political discourse:

I remember one time, late at night in a 'caf', and we were talking about Communism, or more probably he was monologuing, and he suddenly burst out, 'My God, you don't know the difference between Lenin and Stalin!' Of course I replied with dignity that I *knew* that as well as he did; but I have a nasty feeling now that he may have been right; anyway, I'm sure I was deplorably ignorant about all the most important Facts of Political Life.

When he proposed, I had the giggles very badly, which of course was wounding, but the idea seemed so absurd as well as unexpected. At all events, Philip was very soon well away with my successor.

Had Juliet but known, there were actually two co-existent successors: Julia Strachey, fifteen years older than Philip, and eighteen-year-old Isabel Campbell.*

To me, Julia Strachey – charming, gifted, and ultimately tragic – was a distant glamour-figure. I never knew her well, although she sometimes came to visit when Philip was staying in Rotherhithe Street. Niece of Lytton Strachey, a brilliant but erratic writer, she seemed to bridge the gap between our generation and that of the fading Bloomsbury era.

Forty-five years later, reading Frances Partridge's stunning *Julia* published in 1983, I grieved for the Julia I had scarcely known. Her letters to Mrs Partridge about her affair with Philip are full of astute observation. From Ebbesbourne Wake, where they had gone for an illicit tryst, she wrote (19 April 1938):

> Toynbee is a real duck, with a good dash of goose thrown in, for which I like him none the worse. He worked six hours a day as he wants to get a first it seems next term at Oxford. In the afternoons we went out, and after dinner we read aloud.

She describes their fish and chips suppers bought in the fish shop for fourpence, or pork pies and sausage rolls eaten in a

* Not her real name. A pseudonym used by Philip in *Friends Apart* adopted here throughout for the sake of consistency.

pub 'to the strains of "Little Old Laydee" or "Goodnight my Love" '.

In the same letter:

> Esmond Romilly and Decca came down (with the baby and all) and stayed one weekend. That was very strange. Somehow I really had forgotten the world at twenty years of age, and it was most curious being thrown into it again. The main horror of young people is that they can't foresee any of the snags that lie ahead, and go blundering along.

Stranger yet, I had totally forgotten that weekend and try as I might cannot dredge it up in my memory. I can only suppose that it got submerged in the general amnesia that set in following the misery of the baby's death a few weeks later.*

Philip described this visit in his diary:

> We were having tea when Es and Decca arrived. I found them very boy and girlish, walking thru the fields, Es lifting his plump and v. pretty Decca over all the gates.
>
> Julia and I were more sedate and I felt a little self-conscious. I read the novel after dinner and as usual got gt praise from the dear Roms.
>
> That night J and I discussed them in whispers, they in our old room and we in a smaller one next door. 'Like colts!' J said, but she liked them v. much. Decca she thought affected (on her 2nd level of course) and v. Mitfordy, not v. deep. Es she was most impressed by – his bonhomie *at once* with Mrs Walker.†

The next day's entry relates that we had tea in Salisbury:

> Decca to a car park attendant: 'I say! I wonder if you can tell me where we can get some delicious tea!' She's *not* affected in the least, tho'; it all comes through thoroughly naturally to her.‡

---

* Discussed in *Hons and Rebels.*
† The landlady.
‡ In *Friends Apart*, Philip places this incident in Birmingham.

My sister Debo's coming out dance, held on 23 March 1938 must have been – as balls are supposed to be – a climacteric in these all-absorbing affairs of the heart. The day before the dance Philip wrote in his diary:

> I was terribly excited about Juliet – still am, as I sit here at tea-time. Goodness! How I could love her! But it *won't* happen, somehow it *won't* happen. But tomorrow at Debo's dance (Debo said to Decca: 'I do *hope* Philip won't be drunk!') I shall ask Juliet to marry me again, if I get a chance. And if she accepts, it will be far from wonderful. I shall have to tell Julia about it, and I shan't be able to go away with her.

The next several entries evoke as background music 'After the Ball is Over' played softly offstage.

Somebody gave Juliet and Philip a lift home:

> I was deposited in Oxford Square and she ran into her house with the flimsiest of goodbyes. Raging and ranting I groped my way home . . . it was all so different from last night. If she knew how bloody lucky she is that I ever asked her to marry me. I hadn't asked her again; it was never suitable.

But the same evening: 'I talked and danced a lot with Isabel Campbell, who is charming and only *just* dull.' Next night:

> The Henley dance was unqualified fun. Danced with Juliet, all my rage evaporated, v. affectionate, and with Isabel Campbell. I began to like this Isabel more and more – only 18 but sweet and cultured and amusing.

The day after the Henley dance Philip and Julia Strachey left for their planned country idyll, evidently a huge success:

> Julia was lovely, lovelier in bed than anybody I've ever dreamed of . . . sometimes she just looks lovable and dear, and at others wonderfully beautiful . . . peaceful and wise, and adult and loving! . . . We lay exhausted on the bed, hugging

and kissing. I was wildly attracted by Julia – far more passionate than she was. (26 March.)

   But in the midst of these torrid goings-on, desire for Isabel
intruded: 'I've thought a great lot about Isabel and more or less
decided that I'll try to marry her! Which shows how young
and mad I really am.'
   By early April, Philip was back in London: 'I find myself
insanely wondering whether to try to marry her [Isabel] or
Juliet!' (4 April.) 'As I walk in the spring sun I usually think of
Isabel, and *pray* that I'll fall in love with her.'
   Eventually the Campbells asked him to dinner. 'Lady
Campbell is a nice no-nonsense sort of woman – perhaps *too*
no-nonsense.' Isabel was 'delightful in every way so far as I can
see. But I just don't know her. It struck me that one can't *really*
love someone until one knows them . . . '
   Esmond and I never knew, at the time, of Philip's marital
designs upon Juliet: and soon talk of his impending marriage
to Isabel dominated our discussions with Philip. He proposed
and was accepted; now he and Isabel were formally engaged,
or so Philip believed. But he had reckoned without the
'no-nonsense – perhaps *too* no-nonsense' Lady Campbell and
her husband, Sir Roderick, whose plans for their daughter did
not include marriage to this 'wild and dissolute young man', as
Lady Campbell described Philip to an acquaintance.
   Isabel was one of the 'Liberal Girls,' a coterie described by
Philip in *Friends Apart*, consisting of the offspring of England's
famous Liberal families: Asquiths, Bonham-Carters, Sin-
clairs. Laura Bonham-Carter was an early love of Philip's; her
sister Cressida married Jasper Ridley. Esmond and I never met
them, for they were securely tucked away in Philip's Jasper
Ridley pigeon-hole. 'They were as different from Decca as a
Christian Socialist is from a nihilist with a bomb,' he wrote.
'But they were nevertheless in gentle revolt against the still
more sedate intentions of their parents.'

Sir Roderick was a Liberal politician; Lady Campbell, a Liberal hostess. Their tactics in detaching Isabel from her unsuitable fiancé were Liberal tactics; not for them the strong-arm methods employed by my father in pursuing an identical goal in the case of Esmond and me.

With the Campbells, persuasion was all; to my surprise and Esmond's dismay, it worked. We had moved from Rotherhithe Street to a rented room near Marble Arch. Sometimes we lent our room to Philip and Isabel for a private assignation, which meant going to a double feature film followed by a fish-and-chips supper in order to give time for the romance to bud and flower. But it never did. 'Isabel charming and only *just* dull,' Philip's diary records; privately, I thought her *very* dull, and rather tiresome – although I shouldn't have dreamed of saying so to the lovestruck Philip. To me, she seemed to be a wishy-washy girl with no determination or mind of her own; but this may have been the dubious assessment of an experienced Older Woman, aged twenty, of somebody two years younger.

In *Friends Apart*, Philip describes Isabel in generous terms:

> With her round, sparkling and innocent face, her gentle moral fervour, she seemed to offer all the good qualities which I had failed to discover in myself . . . The Romillys found it impossible to understand a girl who was both timid and stubborn, young in her manner but mature in her common sense. And I danced rather miserably between them, protecting Isabel when Esmond became too forceful, opposing her, in a conciliatory way, when she refused even to take his recommendations seriously.

As I remember these encounters, I did my best to impart to Isabel my expertise in running away, to fire her with its possibilities. But the round, innocent face failed to sparkle at the thought.

In September 1938, I turned twenty-one, and received an

unexpected windfall of £100, a sum saved by my mother for each of her children in a special Post Office account into which she paid sixpence a week per child from the date of its birth.

The hundred-pound bonanza happened to coincide in time with the Munich accord, the betrayal by Neville Chamberlain of any hope of collective security with Russia against the Nazis. War now seemed inevitable. Esmond and I decided to use the money for a brief look at America, then a comparatively unknown land; we knew few people who had ventured in that direction. But the cost of a one-way ticket was only £18 apiece, which would leave plenty of money to live on whilst finding jobs.

Esmond decided that we could make a good living lecturing in America. He drew up a prospectus for a lecture agency, which began: 'Dear Sirs: King George and Queen Elizabeth are not the only people leaving these shores for America this year. We are also coming.' The 'we' was to include Philip and Isabel – what more perfect opportunity for running away? Philip's lecture topics were listed as 'Sex life at Oxford University', and, as a Father's Day special, 'Arnold Toynbee: Historian, but First and Foremost "Dad" '. Isabel was to lecture on the private lives of English politicians. 'Though by then I was in my usual state of punch-drunk fascination,' Philip writes in *Friends Apart*, 'the picture of Isabel describing her father's breakfast sulks to an audience in Wyoming brought me for a moment to my senses and made me laugh.' But Isabel, 'timid and stubborn' as ever, hung back, and despite all our urgings finally refused to cooperate in these carefully-prepared getaway plans.

Inevitably, the engagement began to unravel; soon it was over. Isabel gloomily admitted that she no longer loved Philip. 'On the next day I dragged this dreadful news about London, like a repellent bone to lay at the feet of my friends.' He was indeed the very picture of misery; I remember him lying on our bed, abandoned to shaking sobs – a display of emotion to which I was unaccustomed, and of which I did not altogether approve, especially when lavished on the unworthy Isabel. As Philip recalled that scene: 'Decca, her brow wrinkled in an effort to understand and to sympathize, said: "Poor Philip, I feel that you're terribly sort of depressed." I was soon laughing at their endearing inability to understand.'

Esmond and I got our visas to America, after the usual difficulties endemic, to us, of dealings with consular authorities. We begged Philip to come with us to the Land of Opportunity; sometimes he seemed to waver, but in the end he declined. I never quite knew why, until I read in *Friends Apart*:

> I couldn't confidently envisage a long adventure alone in the company of the Romillys. My personality, already depleted by guilt and loss, could have been obliterated in their tremendous company, and without another companion to support me against their undeliberate but crushing domination.

He did, however, come to our farewell party held unsuitably in 4 Rutland Gate Mews, downstairs from my parents' house in 26 Rutland Gate, then let to Ann Farrer, a year older than I, who was starting her career as an actress.

'And as that party grew noisier and noisier through the night, Esmond was always hoping that the "Nazi baron" would come knocking at the door to make a protest,' Philip writes. He describes the assembled guests – 'all the odd strata of the Romillys' social life.' (Who were they? Of my family, only my brother Tom came, bringing with him a rare beauty, Janetta Woolley, aged perhaps fifteen – cradle-snatched, I could see – I think I did ask her how she ever got away; climbed out of the nursery window? Quite so, she said. She was to figure in Philip's later life when she was married to Robert Kee.)

Eventually Esmond and I 'became bored,' Philip writes, 'and left their guests to shout and drink without them.' All true, no doubt. What I chiefly remember is a large pool of Toynbee vomit in the sitting room. My cousin Ann was meticulously neat and tidy – 'so *clean*, like a little cat', my mother once said of her – so I didn't quite know what to do about this mess. Being in something of a rush to get ready to go to America, I covered it with sheets of newspaper, hoping that she wouldn't notice it. But she did, as I learned decades later.

Esmond and I left the next day, seen off by an incongruous threesome: my nanny, still worrying about my ability to cope in America – 'those nasty earthquakes! You can't get a proper cup of tea there,' Tom, and Philip.

> I hope I wasn't a gloomy influence [Philip wrote], for certainly I felt as low as could be – the bright sun and the bright Romillys off to the bright USA . . . 'Goodbye, Es! Goodbye, Decca' from the platform. 'I'll send you the next act of the show', and the train was steaming out. I went home to be told by my long suffering mother that I was mad, a bore and too selfish to keep her sympathy. This, it seemed, was where Esmond had come into my life, five years before.

CHAPTER 3

Wartime

Esmond and I lived in New York for a few months in the spring of 1939; we toured New England; we moved briefly to Washington, and eventually wound up as part-owners of a bar in Miami. As months went by, during which we were greedily exploring the possibilities of the New World, correspondence with English friends tended to dry up. But in March 1940, Esmond wrote to Philip:

> Why the devil don't you write & what's all this talk about your being married and a private in the Army or both! Please understand that our position on this is that we paid our money for our seats and we don't expect to be cheated of the rest of the show.
>
> For us, we are running a delightful little bar in the centre of tropical Florida – widely known as the Playground of America. What's more, I'll take a hundred to one you'd give a lot to be in our shoes.
>
> Well, do your duty, Toynbee.
>
> Love to you and your unseen bride, Esmond & Decca.
>
> p.s. In fact, I'll bet you wish you'd got that visa, you shirker!

This elicited an answer from Philip filling us in with the latest: his marriage, the war as seen from his vantage point, his final severance from his erstwhile party.

                                        28 Hyde Park Gardens, W.8.
April 2.

Act IV. Scene IV.

Moving as I now do, in rich and rather fastidious circles you will understand that I hardly like to renew relations with my rotten meat merchants. But for old time's sake here is the latest installment of a great human drama.

A wedding was celebrated at the Paddington registry office on the 25th November, 1939, between Philip, son of Professor Arnold Toynbee, and Anne, second daughter of Colonel George Powell. The bride wore a snaky ermine dress, heavy diamond necklaces and a skunk coat. The bridegroom wore grey flannel trousers and a gym cinglet.

A lot of this is TRUE. How shall I describe my wife! She is nineteen years old, blond, beautiful . . . you would both like her. When I asked her father for his daughter's hand, he said: 'It's wather embawassing, ye know. I've only met you four times and you were dwunk thwee of them.' Actually he'd ordered me off a pleasure steamer in the Thames for singing in the middle of a party he was giving. My mother in law is Mayfair-Bloomsbury, nice, intelligent and gloriously rich. Her husband lives on her, and I live on her daughter. This sounds bitter. It isn't meant to be, but at the moment the position is a little uncomfortable. I wanted to go into a sissy A.A. battery run by Victor Cazalet, but my parents in law financially blackmailed me into the Welsh Guards. Not that I'm actually a soldier at all yet. I join the officer's training unit of the Brigade of Guards some time in June. Really I've been extremely lucky to keep out so long. I cleverly enlisted at the beginning of the war, thus avoiding conscription.

Well, you certainly chose wisely. The war is nothing but butter rations, black-out, universal boredom and irritation. The first day or two acquired a spurious excitement owing to a succession of mistaken air-raid alarms. Since then there's been no excitement at all. What's so doubly infuriating for me is that I'm now very happily married and tolerably well-off. If it was'nt for the war we'd go to America, the South Seas, Tokio . . . Anne is the best sort of debutante, with all their fine qualities of ease and comfort, combined with an amazing absence of conventionality. The world would be our oyster.

Last summer was the gloomiest time for me. Having no job or money I only just managed to get enough money by my wits to get drunk every night. There were a succession of melodramatic scenes with Isabel, culminating in my shrieking that she was a bloody little bitch, in the foyer of Covent Garden . . .

There are a few amusing things, such as well-known pansies mincing into the Cafe Royal in battle-dress. In Cazalet's battery a gunner was asked to write an official report on the visit of some officer or other. He began it: 'We were visited by Captain –. He was an absolute charmer.'

Politically I'm fed up to the back teeth with everything. A week or two ago I wrote a letter to the N.S and N. urging all Party members to secede. A few days later I met G.C.,* and all he said was: 'I don't know you.' Silly little bastard! At the same time living with my parents-in-law, amiable tho' they are, has quite disillusioned me about the glamour of the upper classes. Even tho' I can now say: 'My sister-in-law, Lady Glenconner!'

I am quite well in with this new monthly called *Horizon*, run by Stephen [Spender] and Cyril Connolly. They're rather too fond of fancying themselves an island of culture in the middle of anarchy; but I find their hopelessness rather sympathetic. My father-in-law (how you would love his appearance, brilliant red face, supernaturally large, bristling grey hair, jet blue eyes) bores me about politics every evening after dinner. In his time he was a bit of a lad, a member of the Turf Club, a heavy gambler and drinker. But five years as a conservative backbencher has turned him into the worst sort of bore. 'Now Philip, I don't want you to wun away with the idea that I'm a blimp . . .' If he only realized it, his one point is that he *is* a blimp.

The debs are still around, a slightly different crop. But I've

* Oxford friend and member of the Communist Party.

kept a sort of hide-out in Fitzroy Square where it's possible for us to retire into the idle, drunken past. Actually we are now succeeding in going to the south of France for the remaining two months. As you see I've managed the war more ably than most people.

I think that's most of my news. You both appear periodically in the gutter press, as usual. 'Esmond Romilly and his wife Decca are contemplating returning to England now that meat rationing has begun. It is understood that rotten meat is not covered by the bill.' But seriously I bitterly envy your escape. Do tell me all about your bar, your clientele, your private lives. Tapping the telephone at Rotherhithe gave me an appetite for the seamiest details. I imagine you'll stay where you are for the duration. But let us now arrange an Armistice Party somewhere, perhaps in the annexe of Rutland Gate. Write by return, and I will feed you another scene or two.

Love to you both

Philip

We roared over this typically Philip-ish letter, savouring its every sentence, its every scrap of news. He clearly wrote it to please and amuse us, and to keep up the familiar idiom and jokes; in this he succeeded. It doubtless reflected one aspect of his state of mind at the time – the truth, but not the whole truth.

Thirty-six years later, when Philip was sixty, he gave a very different account of that year. While he found Cyril Connolly's magazine *Horizon* 'a Mecca for aspiring writers' like himself – he began to write for it regularly, Connolly became a close friend, and he had every reason to feel that he was 'well on the way to making it' – there was another side to this picture:

In my private life this had been a dark and turgid period. 1939 had been one of those singularly black years which most of us experience at different points in our lives. So far as public events are concerned, the Spanish Civil War had come to a disastrous end in the spring of the year, and my emotional involvement with the defeated Spanish Republic had been strong, and perhaps deep as well. At almost exactly the same time a much-loved elder brother had killed himself, and a much-loved girl-friend had decided that she wouldn't marry me after all. I was also unemployed during those last summer months of peace; and my general condition was one of extreme demoralization and dereliction . . . *

Curiously, although Esmond and I must have learned of the death of Philip's brother Tony, it made little impression on us – we had not known him, and we never guessed the extent of Philip's distress. In *Friends Apart*, Philip mentions it only in passing as a cause of grief subsidiary to that of losing the affections of Isabel. It is to *Pantaloon* that one must turn to discover the devastating impact on Philip of Tony's death.

Esmond did not stay in America for the duration. He went to Canada to enlist in the Royal Canadian Airforce as a navigator, which required a year's training. I stayed in Washington, where our daughter Constancia (called Dinky) was born in February 1941. Philip records in *Friends Apart* that 'Esmond wrote with caustic pride about his baby'.

In August, Esmond was posted to Linton airbase in Yorkshire. At the first opportunity, he went to see Philip. He wrote to me on 10 August 1941:

> Saturday (today) is a day off, so I came down to Wilton, Salisbury to see Philip – who's now an Intelligence Officer, exceedingly well fed & beaming in a first lieutenant's uniform. Here is no Coventry or Smolensk, but an extremely well-appointed cosy life (Sats-Suns off, the Intelligence Dept. being more like an advertising agency than an army). Small roast pigeons for dinner & continual weekend visitors. Philip's wife, Anne, is frightfully nice. She was conscripted but got a job in

---

* *A Writer's Journey*, Cheltenham Festival, 1976.

the Salvage Dept. right in Wilton. They have a maid & half the house, lots of rooms etc. & a resident Lady Fowler who lives in a separate wing & owns the house. What with the visit to the Toynbees etc it's more like studying hard at a university than a war for me here . . .

Philip had the letter I typed to him in March '40 saying we were in a bar, 'Do your duty, Toynbee,' in a huge place of honour like a small parchment saying you have a degree.

Philip's account of that visit, in *Friends Apart*:

Esmond arrived, only half expected, on an evening when I was on night duty at Wilton. He presented himself at the door of our house with a violent Canadian accent and a secretive reluctance to admit his identity. It was only when my wife asked him directly whether or not he was Esmond Romilly that he dropped his accent and his mystery. This wasn't shyness; it was the same animal cunning, animal preference for concealment with which he had held me off when I'd first met him at the door of the Parton Street Bookshop.

From Esmond's letters to me and Philip's subsequent account in *Friends Apart*, it seems that the quality of their friendship had undergone a subtle change, had become deeper, on a less purely clowning level than in Rotherhithe Street days.

Esmond was full of enthusiasm about Philip's marriage. He wrote to me:

[11 November 1941:] . . . I came back from spending a 48 hour leave with Philip – who incidentally is terrifically improved by his marriage – i.e. he is in no sense a menace any more if you can figure out what this means from all the points in his character . . .

[And again:] . . . Philip is very much improved, and his wife Anne is an extraordinarily nice person & a v. good influence – he's very interested in everything again, not all cynical & disillusioned & get-rich-quick etc. as indicated by that letter of his we read in America . . .

The clowning, of course, persisted unabated, as recorded in this letter (5 October 1941):

> Philip is in extraordinarily good form – though depressed at being continually re-posted to places away from Anne . . . The other evening Ivan Moffat (he was at Dartington Hall and I knew him in the old Out of Bounds days) & his girl friend, Natalie, gave a dinner party in their flat in Soho – a dinner's a frightfully rare thing & this was delicious with chicken & wine & a lovely room. Philip & Anne were there, and Brian Howard & Dylan Thomas & his wife; & Nancy Cunard & a coloured Trinidadian airman & the odd German professor, & it was a terrifically good party. The only thing was that later in the evening Philip & Ivan & myself seemed to form into a mutual admiration clique consisting of each one doing a terrific act & never pausing without giving an opening for the next one. At the end of each act, the other two would say 'Brilliant, brilliant, Ivan, brilliant,' & he'd reply, 'Come on, now, Philip . . . All right, Philip has the floor' so one or two of the other guests thought they had a rather thin time, but most people enjoyed it enormously.

For his part, Philip was at first uncertain as to how the old relationship could be resumed after two years in which life had changed so much for both of them. 'The "show", I now hoped was over, and I would no longer be able to entertain him with my confusions and humiliations,' he wrote in *Friends Apart*. He need not have worried, for Esmond 'at once began to chatter as if we had last seen each other only on the day before. It was no longer nostalgia that I felt, but present joy in acquiring again what I had lost.'

Politically, the two of them were fairly much in tune. Esmond – 'still, or again, a communist, in his old unconstricted sense of the word' – had accommodated to the necessity, as he saw it, of submitting to hated traditional military discipline while campaigning against the odious class distinctions between officers and men. 'He seemed to regard the war only as a necessary but wasteful prelude to the social revolution, and his mood was more directly political than it had been at any time since the battle of Boadilla.'

Philip detected a mellowing in Esmond's political views. In one of their walks at Wilton, 'he told me that his only political motive was his dismay at human unhappiness.' Philip was somewhat alarmed at his confession of this sentiment: 'No earlier Esmond would have allowed himself to be so emotionally forthright, and I had a sudden superstitious fear that by admitting his own goodness of heart he had made himself vulnerable; that this, without his knowing it, might be a preparation for his own death.'

Soon after this he had an 'eloquent, ironic and depressing' letter from Esmond describing his dismal return to the station, where he discovered that his five closest friends were missing. He had spent hours in a plane over the North Sea searching for them. None were found.

> One is really so utterly untough (he wrote) that one is prepared to throw it all over for the sake of a good cry . . . The trouble here of course is that although (rationally) one has faced with equanimity the prospect of death for almost everyone, should it be found necessary, yet we are leading such a genteel life with our eggs and bacon and morning papers . . .

Philip's reply illuminates again the more serious turn that the friendship had taken – and reveals his growing fear and hatred of death; natural enough sentiments, later to become an obsession with Philip. Here, too, are his reflections on his membership in the Communist Party:

> 11th York & Lancaster Regt. Bridlington, Yorks [undated]
>
> Dear Esmond,
>   What a horrible return you had. I don't quite agree about the ultimate merits of 'a good cry' and 'all for the cause.'

I don't think anyone can cope with death – least of all the religious people who think they can. It's monstrous, and impossible to accept or assimilate – or at least I feel that it will always remain so for me. I *never* feel, well, thank God he died as he would have wished. All that matters is that the person no longer exists and that one (& perhaps the world) is worse off without them. I quite see how badly eggs & bacon go with all this. I do hope that by now you have lighted on some sort of consolation.

I find that our discussions have sprouted vigorously – I'm full of vague new ideas which I long to discuss with you. From a personal point of view I have a great feeling of relief – throwing off a heavy burden of guilt. I mean that a year ago I felt embarrassed by the falseness of my position when I talked to working-class people.

In general, I'm sure the Little Man is the enemy to concentrate on. But he can't be attacked directly: he has been put over much too cleverly. As for the Stephens they are castrated with a) disgust at the whole official attitude to war, b) inability to think of a better. Spain has become simply a nostalgic, rather sentimental whirl – not a practical illustration. That is why I'm glad of my three years in the Party. The legacy is a rooted understanding of the class struggle, which Stephen, Cyril etc. have never had. Without that what is there to hope for, except that the cabinet will be reshuffled and the Black Market cleared up (in N. S. & N.)

Can you get off 22 to 24? Anne is having a 21st birthday party on 23rd & I cld come over to Linton on the Saturday, pick you up. Do try to manage this. I'll write again tomorrow. Anne sends her love. Philip.

Here the correspondence ends. There was no answer from Esmond. 'Two days later,' Philip writes, 'a friend of mine in the officers' mess at Bridlington gently showed me the paragraph which announced that "a nephew of the prime minister" was missing from a raid over Hamburg.'

CHAPTER 4

War and peace

In the autumn of 1941 I made strenuous efforts to return to England with the infant Dinky – not easy, as passage for mothers and children was in general forbidden because of the everpresent German submarine menace. My eventual permission to travel, granted after pulling strings that intertwined between the Canadian Airforce and the British Embassy, arrived on the same day as the telegram informing me of Esmond's death. I decided to stay on in America where I worked as an investigator in the Office of Price Administration (OPA), the wartime government agency in charge of rationing and price control.

Philip faded into memory. I should have loved to have seen him again, for he was often in my mind's eye, and Esmond's enticing descriptions of the 'terrifically improved' Philip, of 'frightfully nice Anne . . . a v. good influence', made me long to visit this interesting *ménage*. But at the time (and as it turned out, for years to come) this was not to be.

In 1943 I married Bob Treuhaft, lawyer and OPA co-worker; we settled first in San Francisco, later in Oakland. Like, I suppose, all those who meet and marry late in life – or so it seemed at the time, for I was twenty-five and Bob thirty –

we exchanged endless reminiscences of the cast of characters who had peopled our former existences. Bob told about his impoverished upbringing by Jewish-Hungarian immigrant parents in the Bronx and later Brooklyn; he listened incredulously to my accounts of childhood in Swinbrook and the subsequent bliss of life in Rotherhithe Street.

Bob thought that Philip, of all the Rotherhithe Street regulars, was the one he would most like to meet – a feeling that was fortified when *Friends Apart* appeared in 1954. When they finally met, they took to each other immediately – transAtlantic brothers-under-the-skin? For curiously, despite their backgrounds which could not have been more unlike, they shared a compatible sense of the ridiculous, if not of the sublime.

To capture the essence of Philip during the years in which we lost touch, to trace his trajectory from the time I had last seen him in 1939 to our next meeting in 1955, I turned to his family and friends.

Ivan Moffat, son of Curtis Moffat and Iris Tree, American by birth, was brought up in England. For two or three years, 1939 to 41, he and Philip were close companions. The war drove them apart; Ivan, in the American army, hardly ever saw Philip. He was discharged in California where he has lived ever since, a sought-after Hollywood film writer. On his occasional visits to England in the 1950s and later, Philip was always the first person he looked up.

I went to see Ivan in Beverly Hills. He had a tape recorder set up for our meeting – rather to my consternation, as I distrust these machines, fearing they may break down in the most interesting parts. Actually it worked perfectly. (The typist who transcribed it did on the whole an excellent job, although she added a few touches of her own: for Rotherhithe, she put Rather High; for Anne in rebellion against her parents, she had Anne in Oberlin, a well-known American college.)

Ivan occupied a rather special place in the spectrum of

Philip's friends, for he alone spanned the gap between left-wing politics and the deb dance scene. Ivan, two years younger than Philip, a contributor to *Out of Bounds* magazine when a schoolboy at Dartington Hall, first ran across Philip in 1938. Both were involved in student politics, centring mostly on Spain: Ivan as a council member of the Student Union at the London School of Economics, Philip as President of the Oxford Union. And it was Ivan who, in a perceptive bit of match-making, introduced Philip to his future bride Anne Powell.

> We knew each other vaguely, but we never really as it were 'met' in inverted commas until we were both in white tie and tails at a débutante ball in the spring of 1939 [said Ivan]. Philip, seeing me there, put on a sort of waggish, roguish smile. He came up to me and said 'Old boy, I can see you're up to no good.' (He always called me 'old boy,' even though he was older than I.) 'I suppose what we're doing here is "contacting." ' And again with a sort of roguish humbug, clownish, hypocritical wink, he said: 'Well, whether we're up to any good or not, old boy, let's do it together.'

I asked Ivan, who had observed Philip in action both at deb dances and Communist rallies in the 1930s, how these disparate activities fitted in to what Philip later came to perceive as a lifelong battle between Good and Evil. Did the CP represent the Good (as Philip seemed to say in his Cheltenham talk) and the white-tie-and-tails affairs the Evil?

Ivan thought it was by no means that clear-cut:

> The struggle between good and evil, in Philip's case, was a very complex one because one didn't know which was struggling with which, you see? Which side of *himself* he was on. In other words, he was the protagonist of both Evil and Good. He was rather like that cabaret performer who pretends to be two wrestlers – but he's really just wrestling with himself, with a differently clad pair of arms. And Philip was always demon-

strably struggling with the good arm and the evil arm. But sometimes the CP was the Evil and sometimes the Good; sometimes the 'deb ball' side was the Evil and sometimes the Good. It all changed round, and sometimes he would double-face in the course of a single evening.

When did Philip finally break with the Communist Party? Certainly by the time of the Soviet-Nazi pact of 1939, Ivan thought; but even by the summer of 1938, it seemed that Philip's communism was

> part of a kind of fancy dress costume. I'm sure that originally it had been something more serious. He was probably taking it most seriously when he was President of the Oxford Union. But later it had increasingly the air of a clownish fancy dress. There was a tremendous sort of false nose aspect of Philip's conduct, whether it was political or social, whether it was going to dances or making passes.

In telling stories against himself, always a favourite form of wry self-mortification, did Philip embellish the more discreditable aspects? Possibly, although this recollection of Ivan's, as told to him by Philip at the time, rings true to form.

On his return from the student delegation to the Spanish front in 1937, Philip was due to give a report of his visit to a large gathering in Manchester of students from various universities, attended by Members of Parliament and other distinguished personages. The conference had been in session for two or three days by the time Philip arrived, a day late.

> He arrived fairly tight, and when he got up on the platform realized that he had lost all his notes – that is, he'd lost the supposedly relevant notes, if indeed he'd ever made them. All he had clutched in his hand was something which, as he looked at it, turned out to be about a girl named Carmen in Barcelona. He scanned these notes helplessly; of course all these very, very serious students were waiting to hear about the relationship between the POUM and the Communists and Anarchists,

what was the price of bread, the nature of the economic
assistance given by the Soviet Union – all those kinds of
specific things.

Philip abandoned his notes when he saw they were all about
Carmen, and started to improvise. He said, 'Comrades, we
were travelling at night in a camion,' – ('Camion', by the way,
was a romantic catchword of the day, signifying solidarity and
familiarity with the Spaniards of the Republic.) He went on,
smiling at the audience: 'And there we saw Madrid far below
us, twinkling in the lights; comrades, you wouldn't have
known there was a war on.'

This, of course, was met by a tremendous barrage of boos,
because it was patently rubbish, and everybody knew all too
well there was a war on; they didn't care whether Philip knew it
or not, they wanted something else. So he was booed off the
stage then and there. He stumbled off, and that was that.

The 'hide-out in Fitzroy Square' of Philip's 1940 letter to us
was the home of Ivan's father who was then away in America,
so Ivan had the run of this large, luxurious flat all through the
war. Philip was a frequent visitor:

He'd come and doss down. There was no question of 'staying'
in the formal sense. He'd doss down on different nights in
different places – 'where I drinks I sleeps', as it were. When he
saw the night's end coming he had a habit of making a kind of
dive towards a sofa or even a soft carpet. There were spare
bedrooms, but he would just curl up on the floor in a foetal
position. As well as say 'I dare you to try and kick me out!'

My cousin David Tree used to have a nickname for Philip:
Plunger Abrahams; 'Abrahams' because of his fierce Biblical
look, and 'Plunger' because he would plunge to the floor,
plunge into this and that – parties, beds, causes. His passes at
girls were in the nature of plunges.

The 'Biblical look' was also remarked on by Robert Kee who
wrote in his 1939 diary, 'Met PT on channel steamer – He
looked like an Old Testament prophet with cirrhosis of the
liver.'

As seen by Ivan, these passes were random, desultory and seldom crowned with success: nor were they intended to be. 'The pass was the thing, the pass was all, they were not really designed to work. The result was unimportant; failure was implied in it – and not always undesired.'

Ivan was a frequent participant in these excursions. He and Philip would meet regularly, once or twice a week, at Oddenino's bar in Regent Street, the ostensible purpose being to have a few drinks, then go out to various pubs and nightclubs to try to pick up girls. 'Though we had dozens of such evenings, we never once picked up any girls,' he said. There was a reprise of this old act in 1953, when they met for the first time in many years during one of Ivan's rare visits to London. They met in a Soho pub:

> He was really much more drunk than normally when we'd met in the old days. We went on to the Gargoyle, and halfway through dinner, to my great chagrin, he suddenly announced, 'Old boy, I've got to go home,' and he started to fold up. I was absolutely stunned by the prematurity of this announcement – it was no later than nine o'clock.
>
> So I said, 'But we haven't begun, we haven't even faintly begun to achieve our traditional objective' – which was to find a girl. He put out his hand in a characteristic gesture: 'Right,' he said. 'That must not be allowed to happen.' He then stood up, went to the next table where a suburban couple were having dinner, stood stiffly before the woman and said to the man: 'Excuse me, sir.' And to the woman, 'Madam, I'd very, very much like to go to bed with you.' Before she could make any answer, he said, 'Now don't, don't say anything. I mean it stands to reason that you don't fancy the idea in the slightest, and on the very face of it how could such a thing happen? However, I did want to register my wish in your regard. Thank you very much.' He waved at me and dashed out.

Ivan must have relished, as Esmond and I had earlier, the ever-present dramatic possibilities afforded by friendship with Philip, for it was he who stage-managed Act IV (as Philip

called it in his letter to us): Philip's marriage to Anne
Powell.

Ivan was a close friend of Anne's, whom he had met
through her older sister Elizabeth Glenconner. 'I liked Anne
enormously,' he said. 'And I knew that Philip would be
instantly attracted to her freshness of appearance, her yellow
hair and her lovely complexion – and the freshness, generally,
of her manner, her intensity, cleverness, intelligence, above
all, sense of fun.' Ivan was confident that Anne, for her part,
would fall for Philip:

> The reason I was so certain was that Anne was somewhat in
> rebellion against her conservative colonel father, and she
> would find in Philip the perfect answer – the perfect terms in
> which to rebel. I was sure she would find him immensely
> attractive in the context of her attitude to her parents, aside
> from the intrinsic attractions of Philip: his sort of ugly beauty,
> like a statue that's been out in the rain. Coming from an
> ordered, upper-class family she would be enchanted by
> Philip's *dégringolade*, his general appearance of anarchy.

Having concluded that these two were made for each other,
Ivan took appropriate action:

> I said to Anne, 'Come to tea tomorrow and you'll meet the
> man you're going to marry.' And I said to Philip, 'Come to tea
> tomorrow and you'll meet the girl you're going to marry.' So
> they did come to tea. They chatted away – got on like wildfire,
> and within a few weeks they were engaged.

The comic potential inherent in this union was not lost on
Ivan.

> I knew that to Colonel Powell, Philip would be the absolute
> archetype of anti-son-in-law – possibly the person that if you
> were Colonel Powell you would least like to have as your
> son-in-law; although I think probably later on he realized that

Philip had a good deal of intellectual substance. But the Colonel's lady, Barbara Powell, liked Philip from the start. She was rather liberal in outlook, read the *New Statesman* and that sort of thing.

Eventually Colonel Powell summoned Philip for a formal interview to question him about his plans *vis à vis* the war effort.

Philip said, in typical style, that he thought he'd join the Metropolitan Police; after all, they wore steel helmets like soldiers when they were on duty. Needless to say this idea was, on the face of it, extremely distasteful to Colonel Powell of the Brigade of Guards, former Tory Member of Parliament – his son-in-law a policeman! So the Colonel then said, 'Well, Barbara and I had rather thought it would be a good idea if you joined the Army. I've still got some connection with the Brigade of Guards and we might find you a situation there.'

Philip countered with the idea that he could join up in a notoriously effete battery manned by an odd assortment of writers and painters, incongruously decked out as bombardiers in full battle dress – amongst them, Ben Nicolson* who was one of Philip's best friends. At the time it was said – I don't know with what accuracy – that Winston Churchill had established this outfit for people who were patently not soldier types, so they would be less likely to be cannon fodder, thrown into the trenches and mowed down as happened to their counterparts in the First World War.

The colonel then said to his wife, 'Barbara, would you mind leaving the room?' She dutifully did so and the colonel, looking Philip squarely in the eye, said, 'Philip, I don't think your mother-in-law would much care for the idea of her son-in-law being a member of a bugger's battery.'

Philip must have capitulated, for his next move was an effort to join the Welsh Guards: 'He sort of made a *pass* at the

* Benedict Nicolson.

Guards, the sort of pass that Philip was already accustomed to seeing rejected,' Ivan said.

Predictably, the 'pass' was ultimately unsuccessful, its failure perhaps foreshadowed by Philip's arrival at Sandhurst as described by my brother-in-law Andrew Devonshire.

Andrew (then Cavendish) met Philip in the spring of 1940 at Caterham Barracks where, as Brigade of Guards candidates, they underwent several weeks of very tough training. 'He was a tremendous blessing to me,' said Andrew, 'because he was even *more* inefficient than I was, more often late on parade so that my own derelictions in this respect were less noticeable than his.'

After Caterham the cadets were given a brief leave, and a day off in London, before taking an evening train to Sandhurst.

By a miracle Philip, who had decided the best way to spend the free day was to have masses of drinks, arrived at Waterloo on time – he was very, very drunk. But that was all right, as he was among friends. We got to Woking and were met by army vehicles to take us to Sandhurst. So far all was well, because we were watching out for him, looking after him, making sure he didn't do anything disgraceful. But when we got into Sandhurst grounds – which were very splendid, so were the buildings – we took our eyes off Philip for one minute, we were gazing around us, interested in seeing what was to be our new home.

In a twinkling of an eye he'd taken *all* his clothes off. By now we had arrived, were met by senior officers, and there was Philip on the floor of the lorry with no clothes on. This, however, showed the Guards at their very best. A senior officer quietly gave orders to sergeants, who arrived with a stretcher, took this lifeless looking thing to his room with all his belongings. Nothing was ever, ever said about the matter.

During the four-months Sandhurst training Andrew and my sister Debo, whom he was then courting, saw a great deal of Philip and Anne; the four of them were often together. 'Philip was very remarkable,' Andrew said. 'The military life was *not* his style but he really *did* try. He was a source of great joy to us – (a) he was marvellous company, (b) no matter how ill-polished our boots were, his would be worse.'

Another source of delight was Philip's constant exploitation of potentially comic situations.

> At supper the instructors had to eat with the cadets. In order to curry favour, Philip would sit next to these officers whenever he could. They were young, but older than us. His gambit was: 'I expect you know my father-in-law Colonel Powell?' 'Oh – yes,' they'd answer – and then an incredulous double-take: 'WHAT? *YOUR* father-in-law?'

Philip was unique, Andrew said. 'His most lovable attribute: if one was in trouble, he was certain to be in even deeper trouble.'

Perhaps, Andrew thought, Philip was too independent-minded for the Guards; in any event, he was not accepted, but was drafted into the Intelligence Service – 'much more his line.'

A standing joke between Ivan and Philip was 'Let's be frank,' a useful all-purpose phrase to be trotted out in arguments and moments of catastrophe. Its origin was a disastrous visit in the summer of 1939 to David Tennant, then married to Ivan's cousin Virginia, at Teffont Abbey in Wiltshire. Philip and Ivan hitchhiked down. Walking through Camberley, Philip insisted on making a detour through the Imperial Staff College where a reunion of smartly-dressed officers was in progress. Philip, urging the reluctant Ivan on, decided to infiltrate this gathering: 'We were conspicuous, of course, not only by our dress and appearance but by our ages. Philip said we were

looking for a certain Major Harbottle, on the face of it
ludicrous, and the adjutant soon had us kicked out.'

Ivan didn't find this mini-escapade enjoyable, but he entered
into the spirit sufficiently to telephone a message to David
Tennant's butler who announced to David that 'a Mr Honeybee is arriving by foot, sir.' By five o'clock, 'Honeybee' and
friend arrived.

> Immediately Philip, who had never met David before, darted
> into the dining-room and looked for drink; he had a very keen
> eye for hidden bottles and decanters. He found brandy, crème
> de menthe and things, and put several of those down, and by
> the time we actually sat down to dinner, he was awfully drunk.
> And suddenly I saw to my horror across this lovely polished
> table – silver candlesticks and so on – a great, huge sea of dark
> red wine-vomit spreading. So I said 'For God's sake, Philip . . .'
> and started trying to mop it up with a napkin.
>
> But David saw it, from the head of the table. He said, rather
> reasonably in the circumstances, 'Now look here, Philip, I
> don't think you can really quite do that,' and Philip winked at
> him and said, 'Let's be frank – I *have* done it.'

There is an addendum to this episode. In the summer of
1981, Anne wrote to tell Ivan that Philip was dying. 'She
thought that I should acknowledge this fact when writing to
him, and added "You must also say something funny that will
amuse him." A terribly difficult task.' Ivan accomplished it *con
brio*. In his letter to Philip he recalled shared experiences:

> To think we were Comrades once! Yet perhaps after all there is
> more sweetness than absurdity in that. What have all of us to be
> forgiven for except that there's just as much to be done now as
> when we thought we were about to have done it forever – that
> was the folly. [And he added a PS] Archangel Gabriel: A Mr
> Honeybee is arriving on foot, sir.

Patrick Leigh Fermor enlisted in the Irish Guards about the
same time as Philip's failed efforts to join the Welsh Guards.

They first met after the war, in which Paddy had served as organizer of the Resistance movement in Crete where, disguised as a shepherd, he led perilous expeditions against the occupying Nazis.

This must have had enormous appeal for Philip who had unsuccessfully tried to join the Commandos. He had told Esmond of his intense gloom at being stuck behind the lines in Intelligence. Once more, as when he was a student delegate in Spain, he suffered keenly from living in relative comfort, far from the real action.

The shared interests of Paddy and Philip proved to be the bond that made for enduring friendship: literature, history, above all their mutual delight in people, in the quirkiness and absurdities of life.

Paddy's account of his early postwar meetings with Philip filled me with envy: 'Oh Lord I want to be in that number, When the saints go marching in.' Actually there were more sinners than saints; they marched in to the Gargoyle:

> a marvellous haunt of millions of little square mirrors, like mosaic, a gleaming penumbra of cigarette smoke with a small fluctuating dance floor, and so dark at first that it took time to single out the other denizens dotted about: David and Virginia Tennant, Dylan Thomas, John Minton, Lucien Freud, Brian Howard and Sam, Cyril Connolly, Peter Quennell, Stephen Spender, Daphne and sometimes Henry Bath, Derek Jackson, Robert and Janetta Kee, Freddy Ayer, Ben Nicolson, Robin and Mary Campbell.

The Gargoyle, said Paddy, seemed like a never-ending party. 'It still had an aura of the twenties and faded Arlen-like smartness, now turned definitely Bohemian in character: rather shabby, very informal and tremendous fun – a last refuge after the changes at the Café Royal.'

Whenever he was in London, 'Philip gravitated to it at night like an iron filing.' As at Ivan Moffat's flat, Philip was dis-

covered one morning dossed down on a sofa in Joan's* and-
Paddy's 'topsy-turvy' flat next to Heywood Hill's book-shop.
'He woke up, utterly at sea as to where he was. It had been a
late evening. He stayed two or three days, which we spent
talking and pub-crawling – the Bunch of Grapes in Shepherd's
Market, the Running Footman and several others. His
favourite afternoon haunt was a journalist's club called the
Wig and Pen.

> It was a marvellously exhilarating time: hangovers were
> drowned like kittens each morning in a drink called either a
> 'Dog's Nose' or a 'Monkey's Tail': a pint of beer with a large
> gin or vodka slipped into it, which worked wonders. But what
> was wrong with this was that he wasn't supposed to be there at
> all – or only up for one night, his return to the country, owing
> to all this wassail, being deferred by missed trains or oblivion,
> while poor Anne languished in the Isle of Wight. We really *did*
> try to get him to go back but failed. He was racked with guilt
> about this in the mornings, and painted a comic, rueful but
> affectionate picture of his return, with Anne waiting with a
> huge sledge-hammer on which was inscribed 'THE WORKS.'

These dissolute nights never led to rows, Paddy said, 'but
could end abruptly in collapse, as though a sniper had picked
him off; and he fell like Lucifer. Dylan Thomas's nocturnal
eclipses were slower, but equally complete, and one evening
ended with them both tucked up on sofas.'
Philip's outings to London and the Gargoyle scene became a
recurring pattern. When, a few years later, Anne did indeed
give him 'the works' – she abruptly left him to marry Richard
Wollheim – Paddy felt a bit guilty. He and Philip were
sentimentally recalling those intemperate and exhilarating
episodes. 'Philip said "Yes, it *was* terrific. But I think that's
what really mucked things up" – meaning home life, mar-

---

* Joan Eyres Monsell, who later married Paddy.

riage, etc. I do hope it wasn't only that; but I can't help seeing
that it may have helped.'

Paddy observed that

> the clown side of Philip came notably into play whenever he
> felt particularly strongly about something. Was he really
> sacked from the Communist Party for saying, in an address to
> an earnest audience ' . . . and what's more, if you join the
> party, you'll get all the girls, they love it'? I asked him how he
> had enjoyed the Aldermaston march and he said, 'Well, it was a
> bit of a fiasco. I was rather on the lookout for some suitable girl
> – you know, khaki shorts rubbing against khaki shorts as we
> trooped along.'

In the same vein, Philip told Paddy about a prewar political
meeting in Oxford:

> It was late afternoon: Philip was feeling in no shape for
> addressing that sea of pink faces. He mumbled a sort of
> preamble, then suddenly noticed the clock at the end of the hall
> showed six. He said, 'Just excuse me for a moment, will you?'
> left the stage, nipped out of a side-entrance, hared down a lane,
> turned right, shot into the 'Fox', ordered a double vodka,
> chucked it down, legged it back to the hall and carried on: '. . .
> As I was saying, Comrades . . .'

A side of Philip that I had missed – but that I can well
visualize from Paddy's description – was his romanticized, yet
as always self-kidding, yearning for identity with his alleged
rugged Australian forebears.

> He relished the idea that his grandfather was originally Aus-
> tralian, and his favourite song was 'Waltzing Matilda', often
> yearningly sung when he'd had a few. He had never been to
> Australia, but he dreamed longingly of what it would have
> been like to have been a swagman or bushwhacker on the
> Wallaby Trail; billabongs and coolibahs were full of romance
> for him. When he got to the line: 'Where is that jumbuck

you've got in your tucker-bag?' he invariably stopped to say, 'An idiotic question – it answers itself,' and he'd be off again. He sang very well and enjoyed it, and as I did too, there was often a lot of noise.

He almost, but not quite, led one to believe (or would have liked to) that a generation or so back he sprang from outlawed and vigorous loins between the wombats' holes and the dingo-fence. Misty – and totally imaginary – hints were dropped of leg-irons and Botany Bay, with a dash of Ned Kelly thrown in.

Paddy, who had been brought up on Gilbert Murray's translations from the Greek, rather cruelly punctured Philip's dream ancestry balloon. He discovered in an essay about Gilbert Murray that the latter's grandfather had been Sir Somebody Murray, deservedly knighted after a sedate career of meritorious public service.

I told Philip this, and pointed out that, with his Wykhamist father, this made the convict hulks, the outback and the kangaroos pretty remote.

'*Was* he?' he said. '*Blast!*' He banged one fist into the palm of the other, then his sliced-melon grin chased his scowl away. 'You mustn't shatter *all* my illusions.'

Pondering the web of contradictions that made Philip such a pleasure – and sometimes such a pain – to his family and friends, Paddy surmised that

he cherished the idea of wild, disreputable, and perhaps half-imaginary forebears in the same way that someone dogged by a more conventional romanticism might hanker for grandeur, and leave one with no doubt about his links with Arundel and Castle Howard.

These legendary spots seldom figured in his conversation, although they were to loom large in *Pantaloon*.

The escapades of pass-making, drunkenness, wild be-haviour could doubtless be matched – though minus Philip's special self-parodying humour – by many an Oxford and wartime contemporary. Yet they have been indelibly imprinted on the minds of his friends over the decades – stories to be repeated whenever two or three fans of Philip are gathered together; better copy, no doubt, than the long hours of talk about history, poetry, shared intellectual interests which were the binding glue of these relationships.

Paddy Leigh Fermor ruefully notes that his account

> must seem extremely frivolous, entirely devoted to feasting, drinking, riotous excess and punishing retribution; and I'm afraid it's very nearly true. Each meeting, however many there were, seemed to have a time limit which it would have been wicked to ignore. But there was a great deal of serious talk as well; writing and books and periods of history we were both interested in, chief of which was the later Roman Empire; and there was poetry and reading aloud . . . But much more of the time was, of course, given over to celebration and fun, and it was marvellous and memorable – quite unlike any other stretches of one's life.

Ivan Moffat echoed this thought in a letter to me:

> However much one admired, by instinct as much as by direct appraisal, the intelligence, compassion, reverence for life and – yes – for human dignity – which Philip showed, it was the mischief that made it fun and made it most memorable.
>
> If Philip had been a writer and critic living soberly in North Oxford, with the same body of work left behind – or even more so – you and I would not be in correspondence, and more would be the pity.
>
> Listening to Philip recite a poem, or quote from Flaubert, or hearing him laugh in the way he could laugh in *surprise* if one read something to him that he didn't know about, as, say, from Montaigne – these were the delights which were more often the foreground of those others which form the raffish anecdote.
>
> To listen to Philip in serious argument – and he was a warm, eloquent and vivid arguer – was surely to admire it so much

that not even envy clouded that admiration. Philip's intelligence – and it was a most warm and generous kind – was what
constituted his ultimate attraction to both men and women.

The quality of his laughter was that of startled and delighted
surprise, as if two pieces of knowledge in his head had just been
joined together for the first time to form a new idea – this
pleasurable shock delighted him and made him laugh.

The counterpoint of his laughter was a very eloquent expression of mock pain, when exaggerated disappointment
replaced minor expectations. 'How about lending me a pound,
old boy?' 'Sorry, Philip.' The anguished look – St Sebastian
arrowed – followed by the pitiful exclamation 'Old *Boy!*' in
which reproach was yet combined with the suggestion that
there could possibly be a change of heart, if not of fortune.

CHAPTER 5

Entr'acte: Mummy and Daddy

. . . the children in a fury of revolt; the parents
in a fury of scandalised condemnation.
This was an age of effrontery.
Young men and women wore insolence like armour
And treated their elders like the survivors
of an obliterated age.

Pantaloon

This was certainly true in Rotherhithe Street days. Philip
seldom mentioned his parents except in tones of mild derision.
Mummy, one gathered, was no more than an occasional
irritant; Daddy, a bit of a duffer. I suppose that for most young
people who have just escaped from childhood bondage into
the free and thrilling grown-up world, the once all-powerful
parents soon recede into a backdrop of steadily diminishing
interest – poor, doddering old souls, with their quaint old-
fashioned ideas! Hardly a topic to inflict upon one's contemporaries.

It was only years later, when I read *Pantaloon* and *Part of a
Journey*, that I realized that far from being a minor off-stage
figure of fun, Philip's mother played a super-stellar role in

his life, alternating between adored heroine and monstrous villainess. Thus in *Part of a Journey*:

> All that period of my youngest childhood is filled and suffused with love of my mother. She seemed a wise, strong and tender giantess, holding my hand on a walk or swinging me high above her head; a tall figure in doorways or towering beside my bed. During those years, and probably for many years afterwards, the thought that she might be wrong in anything she did or said was as far outside the reach of my mind as the idea that she was capable of dying. (It wasn't until I saw her dead body, nearly fifty years later, that I realized what a small woman she had been.)

Received wisdom has it that children of the famous endure a special kind of hell compounded of envy of the illustrious parent and guilt for not living up to parental expectations. Was this true of Philip, son of Arnold Toynbee and grandson on his mother's side of Gilbert Murray? I much doubt it. Envy was not in Philip's nature; guilt certainly was, but for his own guilty misdeeds, not for failing to live up to his distinguished forebears. In any event when I first met Philip, Arnold Toynbee, who would have been in his late forties, was just another ageing history professor – fairly well-known in academic circles, his worldwide fame still in the future.

Unremittingly forthcoming with us about his girlfriends, his CP colleagues and Oxford pals, Philip was the soul of reticence where his parents were concerned. But he did confide his thoughts to his diary. An entry of September 1936 leaves no doubt as to his attitude to the Old Folks at Home:

> Mummy becomes increasingly alien. She is such an untruthful person, that's what's unbearable about her. She has a fixed idea of herself which *nothing* will alter. 'I am good' – & that's enough to keep her going for life.
>   In point of fact she's a snob, rather a fascist, an isolationist in every sense, & by no means a Christian.

Also she's a Spartan & has the Spartan virtues, but they're the most lying of all. I'm terribly afraid I don't like her. How can one like a person with whom one has nothing at all in common! Mummy's '. . . quite a humble little person' is typical, & I think literally unpardonable.

Daddy, I've come to believe, is basically right-minded, but abjectly weak. His horror at a very ordinary detective film today was laughable, if it hadn't been such a devastating reflection on all his works.

More than forty years later Philip sent a capsule account of his early life to Ann Farrer:

[3 February 1979]

You ask about my family. Brief resume. I had an older brother, Tony, whom I loved deeply – though we quarrelled fiercely all through our childhood & were as different as c from c. He committed suicide just before the war – the worst grief of my life. A younger brother, Lawrence (Bun) was born when I was 6½, and according to my mother this instantly transformed me into an impossible monster. In fact other grown-ups of the time have spoken kindly of me even after Bun's birth; but there's no doubt that he was loved much more intensely than Tony or me. Our father played little part in all this, except for backing up my mother and generally being rather sour and distant. We came together when my mother left him (for an absconding monk!) just after the war.

Both M & F now dead; Bun is rather a good painter . . . living in our old house in Yorks as a sort of broken down squire. We are quite close, though haven't much in common, apart from booze. My mother became a RC when he was 11 and I was 17, thus widening the rift since she took him over with her but I wasn't having any. Ironically he has now lost his faith, and I make fitful efforts to get it back for him.

I loved my mother to distraction as a child, in spite of all. Then gt coldness in my twenties, but a gradual reconciliation. By the time she died (1967) we were on friendly terms, all passion spent.

I used to put all my sins and weaknesses down to her, but have been learning not to do that lately.

Philip never discussed with Esmond and me his mother's conversion to Roman Catholicism, four years before I met him. Nonetheless, it seems clear that this event had made a great impression on him. Ivan Moffat recalled:

> he always did say that he never threw off the burden, the moral hunchback of what he felt that he was carrying, of having a Catholic mother, and he felt that it made him more guilty about a lot of the things he did than he would have been otherwise.
>
> He used to say that this sort of guilt used to haunt him and when he was at his absolute worst, when he'd done something absolutely appalling like being very unfaithful, perhaps to Anne, and then getting frightfully drunk, he would go round to his parents' house and knock on the door. And I remember the phrase precisely that he used. He said it was 'like a dog guiltily bringing back a stolen bone.' That's what he said, his exact phrase.

In later years Philip and his father came to have a sort of arm's-length love and respect for each other, although their many disagreements of philosophy and outlook persisted. They chose an unfortunate vehicle for sorting out their respective views: a book called *Comparing Notes: A Dialogue Across the Generations*, published in 1963 by Weidenfeld and Nicolson.

What may have been a high point in the father/son relationship surely marks a nadir in English publishing. The 155 pages of tape-recorded exchanges between the two results in the non-book of the year. One can sense the squirming, the shifting in the chairs, the effort to relax as the tape rolls forward recording the Wise Sayings of normally stiff-upper-lipped father and son. The reader suffers along with the participants – and learns almost nothing about the Toynbees as a family; Mummy isn't even mentioned.

Philip leads off:

'I thought we might approach what is going to be a rather difficult job by putting the interview under various headings.'
Arnold: 'Yes, I think that's a good way to start.'
PT: 'Right, well, I suppose the most fundamental question anyone could ask anyone else is, do you believe in God?'

They give God a longish whirl – Indian and Chinese beliefs, Christians, Jews, Moslems, agnostics, Roman Catholics and so it goes.

By page 34, Philip is listing the Seven Deadly Sins – but he has forgotten one:

AT: 'You've missed out Pride.'
[They discuss Pride at some length. Then:]
PT: 'Shall we go on with the Deadly Sins?'
AT: 'Yes.'
PT: 'Now Sloth. That would seem to us a slightly odd one, because it seems rather an innocent failing . . .'

The publisher, perhaps out of Sloth, did no editing of the tapes, supplied no useful footnotes. At the very beginning of the conversation Arnold Toynbee says:

'My parents were fairly liberal-minded, but we lived with an old great-uncle of mine whom you know all about.'
PT: 'Uncle Harry?'
AT: 'Yes, Uncle Harry . . .'

Uncle H. appears elsewhere in the text but nowhere is he further identified; nor are Arnold's liberal-minded parents. The effect is like being at one of those smart cocktail parties where there are no introductions, it being assumed that Everybody who is Anybody will know the other guests.

Mummy comes into her own in *Pantaloon*, in which Philip relives his golden early childhood as adored – and adorable – Fatmouse, her nickname for him.

He and his older brother ('Andrew' in *Pantaloon*, Tony in

real life) bask in their romping affection for each other, and in
their mother's devoted attention to them. Comes the devastating news, as it turned out, delivered by Grandmother:

> Her cries resound again across the lawn and the lavender
> As she moves across the tennis-court towards us.
> 'Lucky boys! Lucky boys! Lucky boys . . . '

And Philip, once he had grasped the fact:

> Called upon to be lucky I went through the motions of joy,
> Danced before the leaning giant at the study window,
> Capered and chirped to him.
> 'Hurray, hurray for baby brother' . . .

But with the birth of Baby Brother, poor Fatmouse was first
displaced, then banished.

> How did it come about [he wrote in *Part of a Journey*] that
> within a year of that birth I was boarding at a private school
> only half a mile from our St John's Wood house? . . . Many
> years afterwards, my mother explained that I had become so
> intolerable soon after the birth of my brother Lawrence that it
> was impossible to keep me at home.

A classic, textbook case of sibling rivalry? Philip never
accepted this facile view of family relationships, nor did he
adopt it to condone his own behaviour, or to explain his
subsequent difficulties:

> It was the fashion of my youth and manhood to remove all
> faults and failings from the children and to place them, like
> sombre crowns, on the heads of the parents. A short-sighted
> manoeuvre, since the children gained only the briefest exculpa-
> tion before their own instructed and devious brood were
> playing the same neat trick on them . . . Thus all, by this happy
> means, can clear themselves in turn of every charge: – 'Not me,
> sir! *Them*, sir!'
>
> *Pantaloon*

By the time he wrote this, Philip had children of his own, and doubtless wished to avoid the sombre crowns that might be placed by that devious brood on his head.

In-laws are a traditional source of distress and bewilderment for the newly-wed; Anne's were no exception. Her own mother was 'serious and humane, a member of the Left Book Club who voted Labour'; she was appalled by the snobbishness and insensitivity of her mother-in-law, Rosalind Toynbee, daughter of Lady Mary Murray.

Philip describes his grandmother (*née* Howard, daughter of the Earl of Carlisle) as 'in principle a total egalitarian but an unashamed aristocrat in her dictatorial treatment of everyone except her husband.' Anne thought Lady Mary was 'frightfully nice', and was vastly amused at the odd mixture of egalitarian/aristocrat: 'She once told me that she had refused to be presented at Court after her marriage in 1889 "because such common people were now allowed there." But her daughter! She was atrocious.' Philip's mother far transcended the mother-in-law of music hall song-and-dance caricature. When he and Anne became engaged, her only comment was 'I can't think why you want to marry him. I suppose he's got S.A.' (For the benefit of young readers, S.A. was short for Sex Appeal, part of the youth jargon of the 1930s, never ordinarily uttered by the older generation.) Anne, outraged by this jarring vulgarity, says that she was tempted to answer stiffly, 'I'm afraid I don't know what that means.'

When Anne's children were born, Mrs Toynbee declined the pleasure of their company, fearing that they might be boisterous and noisy like their father when he was a child. Just as well, perhaps. Josephine and Polly, in their twenties when their grandmother died, have few memories of her, spared the ordeal of grandmotherly visits by her wishes.

Philip, aware early on of his mother's relentless fidelity to her aristocratic origins, played a sly trick on her when he was about fifteen. 'His parents had arranged an exchange scholarship through which a German boy was to spend some weeks with the Toynbees, and Philip in turn would visit the German family,' Anne told me. 'Philip couldn't *bear* this awful boy – Kurt, or Horst, or whatever his name was – whose sympathies, Philip soon discovered, lay with the then emerging Nazi movement.'

One day, soon after Kurt or Horst had arrived, he announced to Philip's astonished parents that he must return home immediately – which he did, by the next train, and without further explanation. When Kurt/Horst was well away, Philip admitted to his parents that he had shed his unwelcome guest by telling him that the Toynbees were Jewish. 'Arnold rather applauded Philip's ingenuity,' said Anne. 'But Rosalind was livid at the very idea that he should have uttered this baseless and supremely insulting lie about his family.'

Jason detected in his father 'a residual snobbishness – or should this be taken at face value as amused fascination with the upper classes?' I should have thought the latter; yet by his own account he may have imbibed a residue of snobbishness with his mother's milk.

From a very early age Philip and his brothers spent part of each summer at Castle Howard, his mother's ancestral home. 'My mother's mother was a member of that great landed family which owned so many square miles of Cumberland and the North Riding,' he writes in *Part of a Journey*:

> My father, on the other hand, came from the professional middle class on the Toynbee side, and his mother was the daughter of a Birmingham manufacturer. It seems odd to me now that I grew up with so many Howard cousins but never met a single Birmingham Marshall except my paternal grandmother herself. The social distinction between my parents was

something of which both were keenly, though seldom openly, aware.

These days, marriage to a manufacturer's daughter might well be considered a stroke of good luck. But Arnold, it seems, never shook off a sense of inferiority due to his humble origins; and his wife never ceased to rub this in. 'She constantly made remarks about his family,' Anne told me. 'For instance, in the war she'd say, "Arnold and his sisters are frightened of the bombs! *So* middle class." '

Polly tells me that after she wrote her first novel, *Leftovers*, at the age of seventeen, which had some fairly salacious scenes in it, she got an astonishing letter from her grandfather:

> quite unlike any other he had ever written. He thoughtfully praised the book in rather serious terms. (I was deeply embarrassed at the thought of him reading it.) Then he came up with an extraordinary phrase. 'Of course Stanley blood runs in your veins,' (a fact of which I was not aware) 'and Stanley blood has always been passionate and turbulent. It reminds me of a current advertisement, PUT A TIGER IN YOUR TANK. Stanley blood is tigerish.' He went on to suggest how different life was in his own youth, and how he might have led a more 'passionate' life, if he'd had the chance. It was the only glimpse I had that this painfully shy, clumsy and often absurdly obtuse man might be full of regrets about all that he had missed and avoided in close human relationships.

She also says that one cannot emphasize enough the full monstrousness of Rosalind, whose bizarre view was that Philip was 'an evil creature – she'd constantly tell him "you are absolutely disgusting", while Arnold, a pathetic figure, weakly backed her up.' Rosalind was also a writer: 'She wrote a ghastly book called *The Happy Tree*, about an aristocratic lady looking out at a tree, her mind on higher things while her middle-class husband snored away in bed.' Tiger blood with a vengeance, it seems.

I never met dread Rosalind, but Bob and I saw Arnold and his second wife Veronica when they came through San Francisco in 1967 en route to Japan, where Arnold was to lecture. We asked them to dinner. Since Philip was the common link – and had arranged for them to look us up – I naturally enquired after him. 'Ah, Philip. Yes. I expect he's very well,' said Arnold, a far-away look in his eyes. 'At least – I *hope* he is,' he added rather anxiously, which put paid to this topic of conversation.

I thought Arnold, then aged seventy-six, a rare fascinator, and his dour wife Veronica, her grey hair pulled back into an unbecoming bun, her manner abrupt, just short of rude, a perfect foil for his almost excessive charm. (Philip used to do an amusing take-off of his father in which Arnold, feigning the absent-minded professor's toe-in-sand modesty, held one hand behind his back while reaching with the other for lucrative book and lecture contracts.)

Amongst the dinner guests was Howard Gossage, a San Franciscan who made his living writing advertisements; but he was no ordinary ad-man. He had the most curious turn of mind, reflected not only in his brilliant copy-writing but in his ability to detect trends, probe minds, explore situations. He and Arnold were chinning together for some time after dinner. Later, Howard told me about their conversation which he found highly mystifying as it had to do with the intricacies and subtleties of the English class system, a subject that he had never before had occasion to contemplate.

To Howard's astonishment, Arnold Toynbee confided that his first wife Rosalind always thought she had married beneath her, and he added: 'Of course Decca, who like Rosalind comes from the aristocracy, has the sort of secure self-confidence that I, from the professional upper-middle-class, could never achieve.'

This made a lasting impression on Howard, and he asked me about it several times. For an American, to whom brains and achievement counted for everything, the thought that Arnold's illustrious career and world-wide reputation came in second to some quirky accident of birth struck him as a really weird distortion of values.

Arnold Toynbee must have been one of the richest writers in the world, his books translated into a dozen languages; his American royalties alone would have been a fortune, as *A Study in History* was 'required reading' throughout the American educational system. Yet by all accounts he was a fearful miser. He refused to employ help in his four-storey London house, causing the seventy-year-old Veronica to drudge away at the considerable task of keeping it clean. If they went to dinner at Polly's house in Fulham, she would have to drive them home. 'To go by bus would have meant three transfers,' Polly said. 'They would no more have dreamed of taking a taxi than of hiring a fleet of Rolls Royces.'

Polly showed me some of his annual Christmas letters to her: 'This is a token Christmas present . . .', or 'Enclosed is a minute present . . .' How token, how minuscule, I asked? Possibly five shillings to each grandchild when they were little, Polly thought – maybe as much as a pound towards the end of his life.

There was a well-remembered occasion when Sally, Philip and their children, exhausted and hungry from driving in from the country, arrived to dinner at Arnold's invitation. They were given kippers – which would have been lovely, had it not been that frugal Arnold served forth but half a kipper apiece.

Philip rather admired this parsimony: 'All the more for me, when the old man croaks,' he would say. But in the event Arnold made a deal with the Oxford University Press by which the OUP would receive the income from his books in return for a guaranteed yearly sum for his and Veronica's lifetime. 'It wasn't out of generosity to the OUP,' Polly said.

'Just part of his lifelong terror that he might end up in the workhouse.'

So much for expectations. Wills are thrills (as my sister Debo puts it), but not on this occasion.

CHAPTER 6

'Being tortured and loved'

I

Anne

A Southern American friend of mine, mother of four daughters, tends to divide the world's male population into two categories: 'potential husbands', and 'not suitable husband material'. By any objective standard Philip would seem to fall squarely into the latter group; yet both Anne, to whom he was married for ten years, and Sally, for thirty, found the experience exhilarating and sometimes delightful, if often disconcerting in the extreme.

Bob and I didn't meet Anne until the middle 1960s, by which time she was divorced from her second husband, Richard Wollheim. There was enormous goodwill all round; Anne maintained an affectionate relationship with her two former husbands and their wives. At the many dinner parties we went to at her house, more often than not Richard and his wife Day, Philip and Sally, Anne's children from both her marriages were among the other guests.

In time, Anne became one of my best friends. She has all but

one of the qualities one craves in a companion: sharp intelligence, quick wit, unfailing kindness. The exception: she is an
unregenerate non-letter-writer. After leaving her stimulating
company, and returning to California, I would immediately
write begging for news of her, the children, London friends;
answer came there none. Once I did get a letter from Anne
written to me in Oakland: 'How lovely that you are coming.
Shall expect you about one o'clock on 3 August.' I answered
by return of post to say that I was preserving this Museum
Piece to be published shortly in a slim volume, edited by me,
entitled 'The Collected Letter of Anne Wollheim.'

In view of this reluctance to put pen to paper, I was doubly
grateful when she agreed to set forth in writing some recollections of her marriage to Philip. I had tried a formal interview,
showing up at Anne's house with my trusty notebook in hand,
but she turned reticent. The interview was on the whole a
failure, as Anne quickly saw when she read my transcription of
it; somehow Philip, in the reverse of fairy stories, had turned
from prince into frog. Actually he may have had characteristics of both, as I saw when Anne sent Museum Piece No. Two.

> I think I was too busy trying to make sense of Philip's whole
> life and then answering rather basic questions to describe at all
> the tremendous fun we had, particularly in the first four years
> or so.

For nineteen-year-old Anne, life with Philip must have been
a dizzying experience from their first meeting at Ivan Moffat's
cannily contrived tea-party. 'I was bowled over by him, and
amazed,' she said. 'He seemed much older than people of his
age today. I was very much in love with him, but he wasn't in
love with me.' (The latter statement is, I think, much open to
dispute; Philip clearly adored Anne, then and later.)

In his long and enthusiastic letter to Esmond of April 1940
about the marriage, Philip touched very lightly indeed on his

own state of mind at the time, skating over it in a few sentences. Anne's description of Philip during their engagement and the early years of their marriage adds somewhat to this sketchy account:

> Philip was in such a lost and uncertain state about everything when we got married, including me. His brother had killed himself, Isabel had left him. The end of the Spanish war and the Soviet pact had finished political involvement for him. The press at the beginning of the war seemed to echo 1914. 'Herr Hitler' had become the Kaiser, the Germans were back to their old tricks, and the people who had felt the war to be necessary since before Munich were sickened by the kind of flag wagging that went on.

Anne, who describes herself at the time as an 'uneducated, or partly self-educated, *New Statesman* reader', must often have felt equally lost and uncertain:

> Philip was embarrassed with his friends at having fallen on his feet by marrying a rich girl at the same time as leaving the CP, so a lot of clowning about this went on, and I had a terrible feeling of insecurity meeting his friends, and being presented as a gilded baby pig and colonel's daughter.

She remembers a particularly awful moment when soon after their marriage they were on their way to York to visit Philip's brother at Ampleforth, and happened to meet G.C. and his wife on the train. Again, in his letter to Esmond, Philip mentions this encounter with C.: 'and all he said was: "I don't know you." Silly little bastard!'

Anne's version:

> C. and his wife were carrying rucksacks. I had a large suitcase and possibly hat and gloves. They refused to recognize Philip in front of a carriage full of people, and to Philip his change of politics seemed suddenly accounted for by my appearance.

So there she was, rigged out in the trappings of a debutante bride, in her own mind an incongruous and inadequate wife for Philip. This uneasy feeling intensified as she began to meet his circle of literary friends. 'When I first met Cyril Connolly at the Café Royal, he greeted me by saying "Philip needed a good woman." '

One squirms along with Anne at the salutation; to make matters worse, Philip seems to have taken a perverse pleasure in her uneasiness:

> In some mischievous way Philip loved discomfiting people, it often went along with the clowning. So meeting all the new friends was particularly unnerving, and I never knew what unhelping hand I would get.
>
> After meeting the older and very clever Oxford friends I would always imagine some very short and dismissing comment behind my back, the minute we had left: 'Mrs Toynbee an eminently suitable bride for Philip, not a totally mindless philistine. Not quite up to Miss—standard, etc.

Such were the inauspicious beginnings, but there were marvellous good times to follow. In spite of the war there were all sorts of delightful holidays – the variety of which must have satisfied Philip's penchant for a life of contrasts – spent at Glen, the noble pile of Anne's sister and brother-in-law, Lord and Lady Glenconner; at various pubs near Oxford; in a remote, weatherbeaten Cornwall cottage. 'On longer holidays, Philip would immediately set up a routine of writing, walking, going to the local pub, from which it was almost impossible to deflect him,' said Anne. It was on one such pub crawl that he lost most of his teeth. Some black American soldiers came into the pub. A local patron began shouting, 'Out, niggers, get out.' Philip, enraged, denounced him for a bigot, upon which the local man asked Philip to step outside. Innocent of the dire meaning of this invitation – thinking that they would merely resume the argument away from the

Philip – a synthesis of all the 'faces'.

Philip aged about 7, carrying his younger brother Lawrence.

Philip aged perhaps 11 or 12.

The Army days in Belgium when Philip and John Bury donned dog collars for their own amusement.

Philip with Patrick Leigh Fermor.
(Anne Wollheim)

Philip at Sandhurst, 1940.

Philip in his rugby clothes at Oxford. He loved the game, and considered membership of the team to be one of his great achievements.

Philip and Sally. (Lucy Toynbee)

distraction of a crowded pub – Philip complied, and was painfully surprised when the bigot landed a blow that broke his jaw and knocked out his teeth.

In London, said Anne, there were endless enjoyable evenings with Ivan Moffat in his father's flat in Fitzroy Square, 'drinking Curtis Moffat's famous cellar before it should get bombed.' (Philip, of course, was the one who got bombed, in the colloquial sense.)

The clever Oxford friends soon dropped their condescending attitude – if, indeed, it had ever existed outside Anne's nervous imagination. Ben Nicolson often came to stay in the Isle of Wight. When Josephine was not quite two, he taught her to recognize the styles of great artists and to say 'Courbet' or 'Bonnard' when shown reproductions of their work.

> The year after Polly was born, Ben brought down a cricket eleven, the 'Town Tigers', to play against the local village team in which Philip played. The Town Tigers consisted of Ben, Martyn Beckett, V. S. Pritchett, Freddy Ayer, Raymond Carr, Priestley (who was a neighbour), Raymond Asquith, Nigel Nicolson, Evelyn Shuckburgh – most, if not all of whom, had last played cricket at school.

Aside from these pleasurable diversions, Anne soon discovered that the chief bonus of being married to Philip was his far-ranging, restless curiosity about myriad aspects of the human condition. Together they read, explored, discussed; this was the mind-expanding 'liberal education' that Anne had missed as a child.

But always in the background was the Demon Rum as our forefathers – and more so, our foremothers – referred to what is now called booze. The demon pursued Philip to the end of his days; his efforts to overcome what is now termed 'a drinking problem' never met with much success. Perhaps his heart was never really in it. For his friends, Philip's drunken episodes were often amusing, seldom painful. At the worst, as

Robert Kee said to me, 'it was very disappointing when he got too drunk, because one was deprived of his presence. The only way he ever offended was depriving one of his company. I never even felt cross with him, except for that reason.'

This rings true enough as a friend's appraisal; but Anne, stuck away in the Isle of Wight with the children while Philip nipped off to London for prolonged binges, did get very cross. Nonetheless she made every effort to make a go of the marriage. In 1948, when Josephine was five and Polly two, Anne and Philip went to Poland together on a commission from Weidenfeld. 'It was a dotty thing to do,' she said. 'He was drunk the whole time. I was thinking: this is the last chance, I can't stick it any more.' And she didn't. The following year she left Philip and married Richard Wollheim.

II

Sally

My first meeting with Philip after long absence, in 1955, when Bob and I finally managed a trip to England, was nasty, short and brutish. Philip was living in the country with his new wife Sally. He came up to London alone for dinner with Esmond's brother Giles. Bob had already gome home to America, so the three of us forgathered. Philip and Giles had long since left the Communist Party; I had become a member of the Party in California. Conversation at dinner was acrimonious and unpleasant; the two of them baited me without stopping, bombarding me with unanswerable questions about what was happening in the Soviet Union, and I by no means held up my end.

It was not until my next visit to England a few years later that our friendship was really resumed. By now I, too, had quit the Communist Party so our discussions of those dear dead days took on a different tone – not that we agreed, we argued a great deal; but more amicably and with more genuine give-and-take than on that difficult, edgy evening at Giles's house.

He and Sally invited me to stay with them in the country. I had been longing to meet Philip's American wife ever since news of their marriage in 1950 had filtered through to us in California. I tried to visualize her; super-glamorous Baby Filmstar? Crashing intellectual of the Mary McCarthy variety? I was pleased to discover that Sally (*née* Smith) was neither of these, but a down-to-earth Middle Westerner, to me after long sojourn in the United States, a thoroughly recognizable and compatible type. I could see when I first met her that she was devoted to Philip (to the end of his days she accommodated herself to his endless crazes and whims), and also saw the joke of her situation in this unfamiliar milieu.

She told me about the early days of their marriage. They had met in 1950 in the super-heated atmosphere of Tel Aviv, where Sally was working as a secretary in the US Embassy. They travelled around the Middle East for a couple of months and then returned to England, where for the first time Sally began to meet Philip's friends: Cyril Connolly, Ben Nicolson, Robert Kee, Julia Strachey. She had never run across people like that before:

> Heaven knows what I made of them all. I was absolutely overwhelmed, stunned. I couldn't understand their rapid-fire talk – in fact I often couldn't understand Philip's conversation when we were in the Middle East together. English people of that class swallow their words, and anyway you don't know what they are talking about as they don't bother to explain things, or to fill in the picture for an outsider.

As a Middle-Westerner whose idea of intellectuals was 'serious, bookish types', she was perpetually puzzled by their propensity for practical jokes, drunken parties, and games played since childhood: 'The Truth Game could be pretty painful . . . '

Sally's formal introduction to this *galère* was hardly reassuring. Philip's friends had clubbed together to put on a magnificent feast to welcome her and celebrate the marriage. As the jollification was getting under way, wine and whisky freely circulating, Robert Kee took Sally aside. 'Sally, at midnight I'll make you cry,' he said. 'Oh pooh!' she answered, 'Of course you won't.'

By midnight everybody was fairly drunk. Robert Kee sought her out. 'Sally, we know you're a foreigner and that you haven't known Philip very long. So some of us thought we ought to explain something about him. I hope this won't upset you but we did think you should be told. *The fact is, he's queer.*' 'Boo-hoo,' sobbed Sally, and Robert, triumphant: 'There! I told you I'd make you cry at midnight.' (Sonia Orwell, whom I later told of this cruel tease, remarked in her hearty way that 'any ordinary English girl would just have said, Oh really? Well I'll soon get him over THAT!')

Sally regaled me with this and other stories of life with Philip when I went to stay with the Toynbees in Cob Cottage, a pretty little thatched-roof house in Suffolk. Philip, ever a keen and wonderfully imaginative gardener, had constructed a maze of yew hedges in the small back garden, a tiny but faithful replica of mazes he had studied in various stately homes, replete with false turnings and dead ends; but as the hedges were only about a foot high, they presented little danger of getting lost.

According to Philip, Sally's American accent created some confusion in this rural English setting. Parcels she ordered in London for Cob Cottage arrived addressed 'Carb Cartage'; they had a dog called Boxer, but the neighbours hearing Sally call him thought his name was 'Bark, Sir!', Which, Philip thought, was a perfect name for a dog. Sally had attended Antioch College as a girl. Somebody asked Josephine Toynbee, then aged nine, where her stepmother had gone to college. 'It's a *very* ancient university,' said Josephine impressively. 'Far older than Oxford or Cambridge – it's ante-Ark, in fact.'

Thanks to Sally, Carb Cartage boasted many products of American know-how then unheard of in the average English house: an automatic washing machine, the latest kitchen gadgets, plenty of ice cubes and the like. Mystifying were the two issues of lavatory paper in the communal bathroom. There was Bronco, all too familiar to any English person of my age, fashioned in the then unregenerate English style of a sort of wax paper, most inconvenient for its purpose – and the nice soft American kind to which I had long grown accustomed. Why two brands, I asked Philip? Surely anyone given the choice would prefer the American product. 'But I don't; I like the tingly feeling.' So it was Behinds Across the Sea.*

* Sally, to whom I showed these pages, took exception to some of my descriptions of the early days of her marriage to Philip:

My only quarrel with this chapter is that you make me look like a country bumpkin, fresh from the sticks! After all, I had lived in New York and Washington before setting out for Tel-Aviv and of course had 'come across', as you put it, a few intellectuals though admittedly, not distinguished ones. A more intellectual, though 'non-bookish, serious' type than Philip would have been hard to find. So I don't think I had those particular 'Mid-Western' ideas you describe when I arrived in England. Gullible – yes (and the Robert Kee story is an amusing illustration of this).

I did find it a daunting experience to meet so many of Philip's friends in a relatively short space of time, given that the English do not go out of their way to welcome one. I am sure I felt like the proverbial fish out of water at first, though soon Ben Nicolson and others remedied that with their friendship. Ben's St George's Square flat became the scene of weekly dinner parties, high-lighted by Philip's brilliant turns. Unfortunately, often the shades came down long before the rest of us were ready to call it a night. Sometimes we played the games you mention, but the Truth Game was prohibited after some too – 'truthful' disclosures caused pain, chiefly to Philip who felt his closest friends had misjudged him.

During those earliest days in England, a more alarming prospect concerned my 'presentation' to Philip's family: Josephine and Polly (then aged eight and four); Anne, Rosalind, Arnold and Veronica. I needn't have worried. They accepted me and our involvement and concern with one another grew over the years.

Again, Bob was in America and missed this visit to Cob Cottage, but our eleven-year-old son Benj was with me on his first trip to England. In preparation for his introduction to Limeys, he had studied their language by reading the works of E. Nesbit and other English writers of children's books, and to Philip's delight trotted out many a gleaning from nineteenth-century schoolboy slang: 'Crikey!'; 'Topping!'; 'I say, Mater, you're a trump!'

Philip was much amused by the unequal friendship that quickly sprang up between Benj and Jason, aged six: Benj the seasoned old hand, Jason the enthusiastic and adoring neophyte, longing to be drawn into the mysteries of a revered elder. Walking along in the nearest shopping town, the children ahead of us, Philip pointed out little Jason trotting alongside big Benj and asking eagerly, yet somewhat anxiously, 'What are we going to do next, Benj?' Philip never forgot this poignant moment, and often reminded me of it. Benj, compelled by his role of senior advisor to think of *something* to do next, decided they would construct an aeroplane that could actually fly. He and Jason assembled bits of wood and paper, and worked for many hours with earnest concentration. (In 1983 I asked Jason, aged thirty, if he remembered this. 'Of course!' he said, adding regretfully, 'I don't know *why* it didn't fly. Benj seemed so certain it would.')

III

Children

Coming from America, where parenthood is taken very seriously as a sort of grim exercise in personal sociology – our best-seller lists frequently invaded by depressing books on the responsibility of 'parenting', – I was fascinated by Philip's free-wheeling attitude to children in general and his own in particular. While he never talked down to them, he had no difficulty reaching their level; it seemed as though the child who lurks within every adult was particularly alive and frisky in Philip, who managed quite effortlessly to penetrate the hopes, fears, sense of fun of the childish mind as few grown-ups can.

For example, he was given the job of setting and judging *The Observer*'s annual children's essay contest. As I recall, his essay questions went something like this:

> *Ages 8 to 12.* You have climbed a neighbour's apple tree and are stuffing your pockets with stolen apples. The owner appears with a huge, dangerous dog and a big stick. Write, in 500 words, how you talk your way out of this predicament.

> *Ages 13 to 16.* Your father comes to visit you at school. He is riding a giant tricycle and wearing an admiral's cocked hat. Write, in 1500 words, how you not only deflect your schoolmates' derision but actually turn this circumstance to your advantage and win their unqualified admiration.

From talking to Philip's children I gather that the combination of marvellous, imaginative jokes and terrifying, unsettling assumptions as exemplified by the essay questions was the hallmark of his fatherly behaviour to them.

What an exceedingly odd 'Papa' – pronounced, Josephine tells me, 'Puppa, like an Italian pope' – he must have been. Curiously, his bouts of drunkenness seem to have made much less of an impression on his children than his cunningly devised schemes, when fully sober, to bring them to a high pitch of thrilled enjoyment accompanied by purposefully injected doses of terror.

I suppose that a modern social worker, given details of their strange childhoods, would classify the little Toynbees as 'psychologically battered' or some such phrase. Perhaps they *were* a bit battered, but from their own accounts the experience was far more fascinating and life-enhancing than the average child's life with an ordinary, kindly, dull old Dad.

Thus Josephine:

> I was stricken with anguish, fear, enjoyment, all at once.

Polly:

> He invented wonderful games, the best, the cleverest, the most imaginative – and he was completely involved himself in a way grown-ups hardly ever are. His games were always more dangerous, more fun yet horrifying, than anyone else's. He devised them and carried them out with total, concentrated dedication.

Jason:

> Earliest memories: Long walks at five and six years old with my sister Lucy in the pram, through Suffolk villages. In each village there lived a giant (each one acted by my father), some good, though weak and vulnerable, others horrible. The worst was the Giant of Groton, who was *really* frightening.
>   Being tortured/loved: 'Arms for tickling sideways raised!' – in a military bark followed by vigorous tickling of my ribs for as long as I could bear, and sometimes a little longer. Great fun.'

Josephine, born in 1943, remembers childhood in the Isle of Wight, where the family lived until the break-up of Philip's marriage to Anne, as idyllic – although she added that this may be a totally false picture.

'Papa was wonderful,' she said;

> He invented an imaginary world called Ponham of which a wizard, Barley, was king. There were witches – Frightenbottom, Painbottom, Ticklebottom – he'd turn into them. Ticklebottom really tickled!

He could be very frightening. Once, when I was about five, he turned into a witch in the sitting room. I was so terrified that I fell against the electric fire and was quite badly burned.

He'd play wild games with Polly. He used to push her pram down hill and then let it go. Once, when she was a year old, she fell out. Papa's main reaction was 'Don't tell Mummy.'

In fact Polly, three years younger than Josephine, seems to have borne the main brunt of Philip's unorthodox methods of child upbringing – the endless games in which he was himself the star turn, a dream playmate who would without warning turn into a terrifying ogreish bad brother. 'This was all part of the way he'd never really grown up,' she said.

Philip and Sally moved to Cob Cottage when Polly was four; for the next several years, she and Josephine often went there for weekends and holidays. Philip loved long walks through the Suffolk lanes, and to entice the children to go with him he invented a whole mythology of the countryside: 'There were magic stones and other landmarks where dangerous creatures lurked,' Polly said. 'Each spot on the walk had a Giant, a Witch, or a Monster, and these spots were their properties, they had to be pacified, kept at bay.'

More sinister was a serial story with two main characters: Barley, no longer the wizard of Isle of Wight days but 'a good man of the land who would suddenly change into the BAD O'Grady', both parts played by Philip. Polly thought that Barley and O'Grady 'had a certain truth to them in terms of Papa's own personality. When he was drunk – this is how I saw him – he might turn into O'Grady instead of Barley. His eyes would glaze, he'd put on a false blissful smile. It was very perplexing to me as a child.'

There were stalking games in which each player had a 'home', the three homes being about one and a half fields apart. 'The goal was to steal handkerchiefs from the other players' homes whilst protecting one's own. It went on for

hour after hour, we'd creep off through the undergrowth –
very exciting, also quite frightening.'

Philip turned everything in and around Cob Cottage into an
object of entertainment with underpinnings of terror for the
children.

> There was a very tall tree in the garden; he put huge nails in it so
> we could climb up, and a trapeze we'd hang from. He had
> somehow inherited two enormous regimental swords. He said
> that – like in King Arthur – Josephine and I couldn't play with
> them until we were strong enough to pull them out from
> where he had planted them. We soon got them out, and I
> pierced Josephine's Achilles tendon – there was blood all over
> the place.

Every game had 'an aspect of terror,' Polly said:

> At least half the day I dreaded going to bed. I had to sleep in a
> study downstairs, all the others had bedrooms upstairs. He
> couldn't resist playing on this fear, couldn't leave it alone.
> He told me there were rats in the study and he was going to
> build a trap for them. He did it, a complicated construction
> with books and a bucket, with some cheese for bait. He put the
> 'trap' beside my pillow.
> He told us that Sally's old grandmother lived in a cupboard
> at Cob Cottage; he'd put on a monk's hood dressing gown that
> was in the cupboard and BE her. When he'd come to say
> goodnight, he was sometimes good, sometimes awful – he'd
> tell frightening ghost stories. Then he'd pretend to leave, but
> he was actually hiding there, breathing heavily. I was rigid
> with fear.

Sally, a loving and conscientious stepmother to Polly and
Josephine, thinks that Polly's account is exaggerated. Sally
doesn't remember anything about the bloody sword-play,
which she would surely have noticed at the time; and Polly,
she said, was never made to sleep alone in the downstairs
study. As Pontius Pilate wondered, 'What is the truth?' Hard

to come by, more than thirty years on, and given the disparity of age between the witnesses.

Polly does recollect that Sally was extremely good to her and Josephine, and went out of her way to entertain them. 'She taught us to type, and made endless delicious mysterious things to eat, such as little cakes called Brownies. Her American relations sent us all sorts of amazing presents – pineapple marmalade and candy sticks for Christmas.' These were vastly appreciated in austerity-bound post-war England, although some of the gifts were less welcome: 'awful frilly knickers,' Polly said. (Come to think of it, when I was five I should have adored frilly knickers from America and should have far preferred them to pineapple marmalade or candy sticks. The taste of five-year-olds must vary greatly from generation to generation.)

As the children grew older, Philip's behaviour towards them took divergent tacks. Josephine said, 'He was sometimes an awful bully – ask Jason! – yet we loved him for his openness. He always discussed ideas with us, ideas were seething around. When I was in my teens, what I said was always taken seriously.' Polly's view is somewhat different: 'He was fond of us and played with us as people do who are fond of puppies. But he had very little real insight to us as people.'

Jason was

> constantly stimulated by his erudition, both earnest and amusing. I took this for granted until very recently, not seeing it as particularly remarkable. Though my father was very intelligent and well-read, I am certain that he saw his gifts and skills as being no more valuable than those of any other person.

What about the bullying?

> The worst episode, which seems hilarious in retrospect, happened in my late teens. I was shooting at a clay gargoyle beside

the pond. He came up and said 'For Christ's sake don't break that,' then took a few shots himself. It was long range, and neither of us could hit it. He got up and said 'You'd better stop now!' As he turned away I took one more shot, hit it, and it smashed. He turned white, chased me through the house, and catching me round the back, got his hands round my throat. My mother arrived, and he let go.

From Philip's viewpoint, a letter to me dated 1 June 1970 (which must have been around the time of the gargoyle smash) betrays the usual parental worry over teenaged behaviour with a good dash of his rueful self-mockery:

> Our main news is that Jason has just been sacked – 'busted' is what they now say – from his school for smoking pot. As Sally and I had been having a go ourselves not long before, and as he was only following his dad's example in getting pushed out, there wasn't a great deal we could say. Still, he *was* an idiot, smoking the stuff in school hours & handing it round too. Luckily his two most important masters – History and English – are tremendously nice and are still considering him their pupil more or less in teeth of headmaster. He has these v. important exams in 3 weeks, so I'm doing my best to keep him hard at work, throwing in the occasional blow-below-the-belt ('*You're* in no position to talk like that!') when he gets restive.
>   Dramas! Dramas! I shan't be altogether sorry when we're too old for them. And how our children do take advantage, don't they, of their parents' wild ways years and years ago!
>   On the funnier side, I'd just written an article for a special number of the Sunday Times colour mag on expellees; suggested to J that he might just have time to squeeze himself in too.

As any parent of several children can attest, one's attitude to each newcomer does change over the years so that upbringings within one family are by no means uniform, are rather subject to the influences that happen to be paramount at the time with Mum and Dad.

Lucy Toynbee, ten years younger than Polly, has very different childhood recollections, reflecting no doubt Philip's own changing interests.

His Giants and Witches still roamed the countryside for her amusement and terror, but by the time she was coming along, 'it was more seeing how far he could go to frighten us without going *too* far.' (Perhaps Philip himself was beginning to grow up by then?) A deep childhood resentment that still rankles was his preoccupation with Jason's academic progress and his indifference to hers, because she was a girl.

Jason detected a 'characteristic anomaly' in his father's attitude to women:

> While he held rigorously to principles of equality, and was appalled at everyday domestic inequality, he had a complete lack of sympathy with or understanding of feminism. Surprisingly, he didn't think it was important to imagine what it's like to be a woman. He found women's liberation slightly comical. Perhaps this isn't so odd considering his background and education.

From the evidence of the women in Philip's life, it would seem that Jason has a point. Yet in fairness to Philip's shade, I must say that I never personally felt slighted by him. To the contrary, it seemed to me that we met as equals, despite the fact that he was obviously far brainier and a thousand times better educated than I.

Like Polly, Lucy told me that Philip's interest in his children waned markedly as they grew older. 'It's amazing how *little* he communicated with us when we were teenagers considering how *much* he did when we were small,' she told me. 'He wasn't interested in us, didn't know us as people.'

But when I sent her my transcribed notes of this conversa-

tion, she modified it considerably – such are the problems that
beset the aspirant memoirist, wanting to get things right. 'Of
course, as young children he spent more *time* with us,' Lucy
wrote. 'But as a teenager, I used to listen to him and Ma having
long discussions about us, and I'm sure he was *more* concerned
about us than the "average" father.' Listening in on these
discussions from her vantage point on the staircase was, she
said, 'one of my favourite night-time entertainments.'

He never confided his growing fascination with the spiritual
life to Lucy; as a child she can only remember his saying that he
was an agnostic. 'He didn't talk to me about his religious
conversion, never said anything about his new beliefs – like his
books, he kept this part of his life separate from us.'

However she was – unwittingly at the time – in on the
ground floor of Philip's ever restless search for spiritual sol-
utions. She thinks it started with an interest in Extra Sensory
Perception, and his preoccupation with the possibility of life
after death – 'He was horrified by the idea of non-existence,'
she said. One day in 1972, when she was sixteen years old, he
took her to his first Encounter Group.

'Papa had seen a notice of it in the *Alternative* magazine,' she
said. 'Mum didn't want to go – but he got around her. I was
very eager to see what it was like.'

Lucy's description of that bizarre gathering makes me long
to have been a fly on the wall, observing this unlikely con-
frontation.

> There were about twenty people in a room. Each was thrown
> an orange. You were to talk to your orange, look closely at it,
> be fond of it, love it – then everyone was told to throw their
> orange into the middle of the room. Next, you were to sort
> through all the oranges to find and identify your own beloved
> orange. Some were a bit sceptical, but Papa insisted that he
> DID know his own orange. Incidentally, he found his first
> Communard at this meeting.

Thinking about this, I can absolutely see Philip first talking lovingly to his orange, then recognizing it – or slyly pretending to – in the random pile; Sally discomfited, Lucy unconvinced yet fascinated by the performance. I can even imagine being there, equipped with an invisible ink marking pen, surreptitiously fixing up Philip's orange for subsequent identification – and his annoyance with me for exposing the whole patently fraudulent exercise.

CHAPTER 7

Excursions into Toynbee country

In the 1960s and 70s Bob and I were able to manage an annual
visit to England. In London we usually stayed with Anne
Wollheim, ever hospitable and long-suffering of us as guests,
or with Polly and her husband Peter Jenkins. A highlight of
these visits would be a trek to Toynbeeland, for which we
made a bee-line on each occasion. They had moved away from
Suffolk into deeper country: Barn House, a mile from the
nearest village, in Monmouthshire; a decision that had been
made under compulsion of Philip's own recognized need to
distance himself from the deadly attractions of London, rein-
forced by the strongly expressed views of family and friends.

Philip made no objection to this conspiracy of his nearest
and dearest to confine him to country quarters; he was well
aware of the alcoholic temptations that dangerous London
always held for him. At Barn House he generally avoided
spirits. While he swilled down amazing quantities of beer (his
own home-brew, 'strong and absolutely vile-tasting' according to Josephine), I never personally witnessed the dramatic
passings-out described by his wartime friends.

At the Toynbees many evenings were spent swapping
jokes. 'Any new ones from New York?' Philip would ask. He

loved those complicated American puns that work back from the punch line, most of which had been told to us by David Scherman, an editor at *Life* magazine. For example: A lower-echelon Muscovite bureaucrat and his wife are strolling along the street when they meet a Commissar, also out for a walk. 'It's going to rain,' says the Commissar peering at a cloudless sky. 'Surely not, it's going to be a lovely day,' answers the bureaucrat. 'Rudolph, the Red, knows rain, dear,' says the wife, hurriedly dragging him away. Or: Q: 'What is the question to which the answer is "Dr Livingston, I presume?"' A: 'And what is your full name, Dr Presume?'

The best was of Dave Scherman's own making. At *Life* (he explained) all the editorial work is done in the plush many-storeyed headquarters in Rockefeller Center; but the photographs are processed miles away, in the lower reaches of Manhattan. One day a crisis blew up: it was discovered that the wrong negatives for a major picture spread had been sent for processing. 'Où sont les neiges d'antan?' Dave wailed. 'Or: Who sent those negs downtown?'

Philip would then move in for his own turn. His gift of mimicry – which amounted to virtual transmogrification – was to me an unending source of pleasure. He had two set pieces which I got him to perform whenever we met. 'Do let's have "Tortoises Sixpence Each" and "The Whistler,"' I would beg – not that he needed much urging, for like all true entertainers he was never averse to an appreciative audience.

'Well, you see,' he would start off in his natural slightly drawling voice, 'There's a fairly drunk man in a pub. He's propped up against the bar.' Philip plants an elbow on the table, his mouth slackens, his eyes become vacant. 'So then a chap comes in with a tray of tortoises.' Here Philip turns brisk and jaunty – he's a business-like young fellow bent on peddling his wares, an imaginary tray held before him. 'Tortoises sixpence each. Tortoises sixpence each. Tortoises sixpence each,' and he offers the tray in turn to several imaginary customers.

''Ere, mate, I'll 'ave one of them' – Philip is now the gruff-voiced drunk, waving to the tortoise salesman and paying his sixpence.

'So then,' he continues in his ordinary voice, 'a few hours later the tortoise man has finished his other rounds and is back at the first pub, looking for new customers.

'Tortoises sixpence each. Tortoises sixpence each.' (He is the salesman again, strutting about, energetic as ever.) 'By now, the drunk is thoroughly sloshed, he's several notches lower down.' Here is where Philip excels. He is barely able to clutch on to the bar, is drooling and slurring his speech. He gestures feebly towards the tortoise man. ''Ere, mate, I'll 'ave another of them meat pies, but not so crusty this time.'

In the other set piece, Philip assumes the *persona* of a county lady visiting her GP. 'Doctor,' says Philip-the-lady in a lah-di-dah voice, 'I've got the most extraodin'ry ailment. Every time I walk, my female organ starts to whistle.' 'Well that is indeed very odd,' says Philip-the-GP, reserved and professional, lips slightly pursed, leaning back in his chair and smoking an imaginary pipe. 'Er – would you mind demonstrating?' Philip-the-lady does so, takes a few mincing steps, uttering shrill whistles. Philip-GP confesses he has never come across this phenomenon before: 'Do you mind if I make a tape recording to send to a Harley Street specialist?' Philip-the-lady takes another turn (whistle-whistle) whilst the recording is made.

'So the tape arrives in Harley Street,' explains ordinary Philip, 'but the GP's letter of explanation has somehow got detached. The specialist calls his young assistant in. He says "This tape recording has just arrived, and I don't know what to make of it. What do *you* think it's about?" They play the tape.' (Whistle-whistle). Philip is now the callow young assistant, eyebrows raised in an effort to look knowledgeable: 'Well, Doctor, sounds to me like some cunt trying to whistle.'

Others doted, as I did, on Philip's amazing ability to re-enact scenes, to reproduce voices. Paddy described his take-off of David Tennant, who, said Paddy, could become both muddled and stately late at night:

> Philip did it to perfection. After a month or two in the Isle of Wight Philip, joining David at the Gargoyle, asked after other topics had lapsed, 'How's Elizabeth?' 'Elizabeth who?' 'Why, Elizabeth Glenconner.'
> There was a long pause, and David said: 'Philip, I used to think that you were a *friend*. Now I discover that you are just (pause) a vulgar (pause) *snob*. I presume you only want to know about my sister-in-law because she's *Lady* Glenconner.' To which Philip replied, 'Steady on, David. Don't forget she's *my* sister-in-law too.' It was side-splittingly well done.

Given his exceptional ear for accents and language, there is little wonder that among Philip's favourite records was Peter Sellers's 'Bal-ham: Gateway to the South.' He would spend hours listening to the recording, then himself adapt the American travelogue technique to a description of his own surroundings. Once when Anne, Bob and I were staying with the Toynbees, almost the whole weekend was taken up with readings from '*Mots d'Heures: Gousses Rames. The d'Antin Manuscript*. Discovered, edited and annotated by Luis d'Antin van Rooten.' This inspired little book, with its scholarly foreword describing how the manuscript came into the possession of the translator, is replete with explanatory footnotes:

> Un petit d'un petit[1]
> S'étonne aux Halles[2]
>
> Un petit d'un petit
> Ah! degrés te fallent

[1] The inevitable result of a child marriage.
[2] The subject of this epigrammatic poem is obviously from the provinces, since a native Parisian would take this famous old market for granted.

Philip set a competition in which we were to take French equivalents of 'Mother Goose Rhymes' and do them back into English, as van Rooten had done with 'Humpty Dumpty'. We tried 'Frère Jacques', and 'Sur le pont d'Avignon', but the task proved beyond us. After hours of concentrated effort nobody had produced anything worthy preserving, so we threw the papers away. But the thing that absolutely fascinated Philip was the enormous amount of dedicated, unremitting hard work that van Rooten must have put into producing this forty-page volume; 'His whole lifetime's *oeuvre*, no doubt,' he said with grudging admiration. (Paddy wrote, after Philip's death, 'I wish I had known that he loved *Mots d'Heures*. It is my Bible.')

These, then, were the memorable diversions of Toynbee-land: endless jokes, games, songs, each of us trying to outdo the others, while Sally, who usually played the role of amused observer, provided incomparable hospitality.

What of politics? Over the years, as our visits to the Toynbees became more frequent, political differences diminished. We were in substantial accord over most day-to-day issues. Philip, always a socialist in the broadest sense of the word, had long since detached himself from any existing party creed; yet he was capable of dramatic spurts of energy when a specific issue captured his interest.

As Peter Vansittart wrote, 'He never lost a youthful capacity for sponataneous enthusiasm or indignation,' and he went on to describe what it was like to be recruited by Philip in one of his *sui generis* efforts to overturn government policy:

Suez, 1956, prompted him to organize a protest march, and advertise a preliminary press conference, to which nobody came. The march itself had only limited success, though at Edgware I collected some extra followers by telling them that it was against a current Rent Act. Sometimes excessive, or a little silly, there was always Philip's unceasing generosity of feeling, an impatience with the merely theoretical, a passion for the explicit and candid.

Eventually Philip came to despair of all existing political systems. In his piece for *The Observer* of 23 June, 1968 about the student rebellion then raging from Paris to California he wrote, 'What they have achieved – apart from a few practical reforms – is a marvellously vivid reminder that our society is insufferable; that all societies have always been insufferable.' The heading to this article ran:

> Philip Toynbee, middle-aged revolutionary, takes a highly personal look at the student revolt and concludes that the young are right to shout
>
> INTOLERABLE!

The latter word, strung across the entire page in letters an inch high, has the authentic Toynbee ring, summarizing his view of the world as presently organized.

Despite his loathing for the Soviet brand of Communism, Philip never adopted the facile, pop-psychological view that Communism and Fascism were two sides of the same coin, interchangeable extremes equally attractive to a certain type of unbalanced, fanatical personality. As he wrote in a review of *Unity Mitford: A Quest* by David Pryce-Jones, in *The Observer* of 7 November 1976:

> Incidentally I don't think it is simply my own communist past which makes me insist yet again that fascism and communism were two very different phenomena; and that to equate them continually, as Mr Pryce-Jones does throughout this long book, is to take a crude and seriously misleading view of pre-war politics. Stalinism may well have been almost as horrible as National Socialism; the motives which led young men and women in England to become fascists and communists respectively were very different indeed.

So it seems to me that Mr Pryce-Jones has got his history wrong, in spite of the numerous survivors of that period whom he has conscientiously consulted.

Our own political disagreements (such as they were) should be recorded in Philip's own voice. He continually faulted me for being soft on Russia. When I sent him a copy of *A Fine Old Conflict* he wrote:

Jan 4th 1977

I read FOC absolutely entranced. As always your writing is wonderfully vivid and personal; and in this case, of course, the material was just right for this particular reader – i.e. I sort of knew it all, but none of the detail. I think the tone is very good nearly always and that you carry it all off with elan etc.

Naturally I also think that you are *far* too off-hand about Russia and its heavy hand on the party. I know you were almost totally preoccupied with very real issues when you were in the CP – but if you'd looked up *for a moment* from your own good causes you might have seen that what was going on in Russia re civil rights etc was just about fifty times worse than anything you were coping with in California, or even Mississippi . . .

This is the heavy criticism; and you'll get a lot of it in the reviews. (Also a drop in my Radio Times piece, completed this morning, and not bad stuff, though I say it. I think you'll mainly enjoy it – well, 80% enjoy it.)

I wrote back to say that I expected he was right in predicting that the reviewers would go for me (which some of them did), and that above all I craved a copy of his *Radio Times* article. Eventually this arrived, its affectionate tone blunting Philip's major criticism so that I did at least 80 per cent enjoy it:

[from *Radio Times* article 1977.]

. . . Her most recent book, *A Fine Old Conflict*, which has not yet been published in England, shows what a tease she was to many of her grave-faced comrades during the long years she spent in the Communist Party of the United States . . .

Needless to say when Decca left the Communist Party she did not do so in that breast-beating, or I-was-Duped spirit so common among defectors from that organization. She explains in her latest book not only that her sympathies are still largely with Communism but also that her main reason for leaving was simply a sense of the party's increasing ossification, and therefore of its irrelevance to the new social struggles which were beginning to develop in America at that time . . .

Critics will certainly claim that the new book reveals a good deal of 'selective indignation' – that disease of the far Right and of the far Left which prevents both extremes from even being able to perceive the iniquities committed by their own side. Decca makes a few formal noises against Stalinism and the American party's subjection to Russia; but the full weight of her furious derision is reserved for the FBI; white racialists; brutal police-forces and other American monstrosities.

The fact is that she has never been very good at seeing much farther than her own nose – though what she sees *there* she sees with a devastating clarity.

CHAPTER 8

The great books

A wonderfully evocative vignette from the Isle of Wight days, as described by Paddy Leigh Fermor: 'Philip pointed to his desk like a guide in a museum, then put his finger on the walls either side, and said: '. . . and, of course, this is where they are going to suspend the crimson velvet rope from two brass hooks, so that the public may shuffle past the desk where all the great books were written, without touching anything." '

Self-ragging as ever, yet with half a wistful eye on posterity.

His early novels were conventional in style, 'the sort all young men write,' as Anne once described them to me. (I was tickled by her assumption that *all* young men write novels; perhaps true in her circles, although not in Oakland, California where I live.)

His first, *The Savage Days*, published in 1937 when he was still at Oxford, predictably dealt with the contradictory emotions that its twenty-year-old author was experiencing. As he told the Cheltenham Festival audience in 1976:

> The main theme was the conflict in the heart and mind of a younger upper-middle-class Englishman between his unregenerate debutante girl-friend and the party to which he had given his *almost* whole-hearted devotion.

One sentence in this very bad novel acquired a sort of notoriety, by being quoted derisively in a book of criticism by Cyril Connolly, and then requoted with equal derision by Auden. The sentence was: 'I felt a wonderful synthesis forming inside me between Ann and the Party.'

This was followed in 1941 by *School in Private* (rated by Noel Annan as 'possibly the best naturalistic novel of a prep school in existence') and *The Barricades* (1943), which explores a familiar theme: the unsuccessful attempt of a runaway school-boy to join the Spanish loyalists.

Philip came to disdain these early efforts.

I should have remembered how much I've hated, and eschewed, all forms of narrative ever since I finished the last of the three conventional novels which I wrote in my twenties. 'And then . . . and then . . . and then . . .' Worse still – 'then I . . . then I . . . then I . . .'

Ever since I began to plan *Tea with Mrs Goodman* – which appeared in 1947 – I've seen that for me the only way of writing is to string together a necklace of sharp occasions and to conceal as best I can any narrative or explanatory thread.*

Philip's next venture into experimental writing was *The Garden to the Sea* (1953), a bitter account cast as a fictional playlet of the break-up of his marriage to Anne.

In his never-ending search for new ways of expression, Philip then embarked on the *Pantaloon* series, which he de-scribed as a 'semi-ironical verse epic . . . I am absolutely convinced that the verse of *Pantaloon* is a new departure,' he wrote to Peter Vansittart. 'What I have tried to do is to develop and change existing media for my entirely new purposes . . . a Bouvard-like procession through all the major ideas and idiocies of the age. Great fun.'

He was confident that the series would one day be hailed as a

* *Part of a Journey*, p. 102.

masterpiece, and he was sustained in this belief by the judge-
ment of fellow-poets. Of *Pantaloon*, Stephen Spender wrote:
'It may well be the beginning of a breakthrough from the
dreary academicism into which poetry has sunk. The study of
the relationship of the narrator with his mother is a triumph.'
And of *A Learned City*: 'With this third volume of his verse
novel, Philip Toynbee comes into his own as a poet . . . this
may well be one of the most remarkable poems of the century.' Elizabeth Bowen wrote to Philip:

> What a toweringly great writer you are. From the point of
> view of critics who are puzzled by you, an inconveniently great
> writer. You crack right through the surface . . . What im-
> mense powers the carrying-out of this conception required:
> and you have them. It seems to me that at no point have they
> failed you.

In a review of *Two Brothers*, V. S. Pritchett wrote:

> Another important reason for Mr Toynbee's success is that he
> has hit on the right subject: the Grand Tour. This cannot fail in
> the hands of a restless, fervent and cultivated writer who
> responds to the gay, the comic and the intense . . . Mr Toyn-
> bee has done a very fine thing.

Stephen Spender tells me that Auden admired *Pantaloon* as 'a
very interesting experiment'. Robert Nye wrote:

> I am in no doubt that *Pantaloon* is one of the most important
> landmarks of post-war fiction in England. To re-read the
> individual volumes consecutively is to realise that here, at last,
> we have something that can be mentioned in the same breath as
> *A la Recherche*.

He described the series as 'talk – swift, spiky, darting, soaring
– about its cohesive host of strange small stories, episodes,
jokes, ideas.'

Alexie Mayor, a friend of Philip's and of Leonard Woolf's, remembers the latter saying in a discussion of Philip's role as an author that '*Pantaloon* stood out alone in contemporary literature; and how Philip's complete understanding of and feeling for the beauty and use of the English language was unparalleled.'

Philip might have been pleased – at least 80 per cent, – by an unsigned obituary in *The Times* of 17 June 1981 that reflects some views of the small but appreciative readership of his experimental work.

Of *Tea with Mrs Goodman* and *The Garden to the Sea*, the writer said:

> These were both subtle works, and remain perhaps his most completely satisfying and successful artistically. Psychology – particularly the influence of Jung – is completely absorbed in them and they still have the power to make much of subsequent 'experimental' writing in this genre, seem facile.

And of *Pantaloon*:

> A formidable achievement. Even now it is difficult to evaluate it confidently – passages of apparent rambling are juxtaposed with areas of intensely concentrated verbal experience – but it is never less than highly interesting.

As for the twenty per cent that would not have pleased him, I can hear him expostulating with feigned tight-lipped displeasure: '*Difficult* to evaluate? Passages of *apparent rambling?*'

He once told me of a young novelist whose first book had been given a long and enthusiastic review in *The Times*. The reviewer had said, 'This is one of the best first novels that I have read in the last decade.' The young writer was understandably overjoyed at this lavish praise, but he immediately had second thoughts. '*One* of the best? *First* novels? And only in the *last* decade?' He soon came to see the review as a devastating attack on his book,' Philip said. 'He never wrote another. He may have committed suicide rather than be subjected to further snide opprobrium from hostile reviewers.'

Perhaps the story of this suicidal young man is apocryphal, invented by Philip to reflect his own feelings. As he wrote to Peter Vansittart, 'There is only one review worth getting, the one that simply says "This is the Best Book Ever Written." '

While his own faith in his lifelong endeavour was unshakable, Philip never demanded of his friends that they share his high opinion of it. He wrote to Ann Farrer (12 August 1980):

> I long ago gave up saying, 'Love me, love my work'; in fact I don't think I ever said this to anyone, or thought it towards anyone. Some of my closest friends simply have no use at all for the work which is still much the closest to my heart – namely, poor old *Pantaloon*. Ben didn't even bother to read it, after trying a few pages of the first volume and finding them very much not to his taste. This never had the slightest effect on our friendship.

As for my own attempts to come to grips with the verse epics, the only one I truly enjoyed was the first volume of the *Pantaloon* series – at that, it took me two or three readings to fully appreciate it. I tried, brow furrowed, to read the others, but found them daunting; a sight *too* experimental for my liking. I should have welcomed a bit of the 'narrative or explanatory thread' which Philip 'hated and eschewed', and always felt cheated of a straightforward, lucid account of his brothers, his travels in prewar Germany, his devastating divorce from Anne (subject of *The Garden to the Sea*).

I had but one conversation with Philip about the Great Books; realizing, no doubt, that I would get scant pleasure from them he never sent them to me. But in August 1964 we were expecting the Toynbees at Inch Kenneth. Having read that *Two Brothers* had just been published by Chatto and

Windus, I sent a telegram: BRING TWO BROTHERS. (Philip told me that he had first understood this to mean 'Bring Rupert and Bruno Wollheim,' Anne's twin boys; fortunately the lads were otherwise engaged.)

He arrived for the holiday with the book and without the twins. I read the introduction with slightly sinking heart: 'A last word to explain two minor but ubiquitous elements in the poem which might cause confusion or annoyance. The apparent anomalies of tense and person have a logic of their own which ought to become clear with further reading . . .' Not exactly what book reviewers call 'ideal holiday fare'.

Determined to prove that I had indeed read it, I pointed out to Philip a mis-spelled word in the lines 'Faces are shrunk, scarred, shrivelled under helmets: Pickled momentoes: walnuts of Lorraine.' That should be *mementoes*, I said. Nonsense, said Philip, it's *momentoes*; but he gave in after we consulted the dictionary. 'Those useless publishers!' he exclaimed in mock-exasperation, 'They can't get *anything* right, even the simplest proof reading.' I asked him to correct my copy in his own hand – it's extremely chic to have the author's own correction, and adds immeasurably to the resale value of the volume, I said. He wrote in the margin: '*mementoes*! Printer's errer, pointed out by Jessica Mitford.'

After *Views from a Lake*, fourth volume in the series, came out in 1968 publishing possibilities for the remaining 1,600 pages of manuscript began to fade. Philip never gave up hope. Despite rebuffs he continued to offer the work to publishers, and he sent copies of the manuscript to other writers, deliberately choosing some whom he had never met lest their opinion should be biased by kindly feelings towards him as a friend.

His frame of mind, compounded of delight in the reaction of critics and fury at the obtuseness of publishers, comes through in a letter to Polly (10 November 1973):

The really good news for me is that both [Frank] Kermode and Michael Wood have written ecstatic letters about the latest chunk of *Pantaloon* – talking of your Dad in the same terms as Joyce, Eliot etc. So it looks very much as if Faber might carry on from where Chatto's left off. (Extra joy: beastly Parsons from Chatto has heard about all this and is fishing to try to get me back. As soon as I'm *sure* of Faber imagine the fun I shall have writing to that illiterate baboon, from whose condescensions and stupidities I have had to suffer for the last thirteen years! Yum!)

Again, five years later in a diary entry (9 March 1978) in *Part of a Journey*:

Another assault of anger and doubt in bed last night when I could no longer avoid mulling over the OUP's rejection of *Pantaloon*. So I forcefully recalled Frank Kermode's great enthusiasm; and Stephen's review of *A Learned City . . .*; and Michael Wood's admiration; and the constant, warm encouragement of Robert Nye as I sent him each of the six unpublished volumes in turn.

Dipping in and out of Philip's life and now seeing it attenuated in retrospect, as through the wrong end of a telescope, I am amazed at his extraordinary capacity for work, an intellectual vigour that never deserted him through bouts of drunkenness, time-consuming friendships, family life into which he poured endless energy; and in later years, assaulting depressions.

During all the time that he was immersed in the experimental novels he was also writing for *The Observer*, where he was employed from 1950 until his death.

The job was originally engineered by his father, although Philip was unaware of this. David Astor, then editor of *The Observer*, had met Philip when he was an undergraduate at Lady Astor's dances, and thought him 'enormously engaging'. (Did Esmond and I know that Philip was hob-nobbing

with the infamous Cliveden Set? I think not, as I don't
remember the violent arguments, or extremes of teasing, that
such information would surely have provoked.)

> I knew Arnold Toynbee quite well, as he worked with my
> father [David told me]. He got in touch with me – very
> apologetically – to say that Philip was going through a bad time
> after his break-up with Anne, and was there anything I could
> do? There was only *one* thing I could do, and that was to offer
> Philip a job on *The Observer*. He never knew that this was a
> result of his father's proposal. I approached him as though the
> idea had come from me.

Philip came on the staff as a journalist, his first assignments
being home news stories. Soon, David sent him to Israel:

> He had enormous curiosity about the infant Jewish state. His
> stories were excellent, he picked up the knack of news writing
> straight off. I had been more than a little nervous about taking
> him on because although he had published several novels, his
> credentials as journalist were nil. To break through the distinct
> division that then obtained between literary writing and news
> reporting was highly experimental. The experiment was, in
> this case, a real success.

Philip's permanent niche as reviewer came later. Terence
Kilmartin, literary editor of *The Observer*, described their
relationship for some thirty years as 'both professional and
personal. This made it in some ways unique – perhaps unique-
ly difficult,' he said.

> I was in a sort of way his boss – that's how he liked to put it
> anyway, with a tug at his forelock – though in fact I was merely
> the chap who sent him books to review and corrected his
> spelling and punctuation, occasionally pointing out a minor
> factual error. As far as I was concerned he was an admired, even
> revered contributor and I was simply the man who received
> and processed his stuff and put it into the paper. Perhaps at

times – though I was a few years younger – the relationship was closer to that of a schoolmaster with an outstandingly brilliant pupil or an uncreative don with a wayward genius of a student.

The qualities that

> made him at his best such an admirable reviewer [said Terrry], were absolute independence of judgment uncluttered by snobbery or jobbery or fashion, combined with immense curiosity and excitement about areas of knowledge he wasn't wholly familiar with.
>
> For someone so deeply thoughtful he had great natural facility as a writer. He never failed to deliver on time and had none of the touchiness, the temperamental prima donna-ishness which in my experience are the hallmarks of the second rate.

As an example of Philip's deft puncturing of 'the pretentious, the phoney, the intellectually shoddy', Terry cited his review of a book about Dylan Thomas. Quoting the author's words, 'Thomas led what Patrice de la Tour du Pin calls the dedicated life of the poet,' Philip commented: 'This reminds me that he also drank a great deal of what Sacheverell Sitwell calls beer.'

Like David Astor, Terry was continually impressed and surprised by Philip's dedicated professionalism:

> For someone superficially so untidy and disordered he was remarkably efficient and professional. I have seen him, under pressure, sit down at a type-writer and produce a sizeable article in beautifully polished prose in the time it took him to type it. His typing was fast if inaccurate, his spelling eccentric, his handwriting illegible.

(Speaking for myself, I rather cherished these eccentricities: the curious up-and-down typewriting, his idiosyncratic rendering of 'is'nt', 'would'nt', etc. which I have tried to preserve when quoting his letters.)

He hoped to look like a figure from Goya – until he
realised that he had forgotten to move the car!

Fishing was the only passion that lasted throughout
Philip's lifetime. Photo from pre-commune days in the
early 1970s.

Philip at Oxford, aged 20–21.

Philip.
(Anne Wollheim)

Barn House in the pre-commune days.

Front, left to right: Decca Mitford, Anne Wollheim, Philip Toynbee, Sally Toynbee. *Back:* Terence and Joanna Kilmartin. (Bob Treuhaft)

A gathering of a few ex-commune members at the local pub well after the commune had disbanded (1981).

Philip offering fish to the author, Inch Kenneth.

Sailing days. Philip had his own little boat in the Bristol Channel.
This isn't his boat, though – he would never have flown the flag!

I had a ringside seat at one of these virtuoso performances when staying at Barn House in 1962. Early one Saturday morning there was an urgent telephone call from *The Observer*. Philip came back to report. 'Faulkner croaked yesterday,' he said. 'I've got to telephone in an obit before noon, so it can be in tomorrow's paper. Do you know anything about Faulkner?'

Not much, I said. That is, he wrote a celebrated series of books about an imaginary county in Mississippi. It began with Y – unpronounceable; and had to do with a family called – Scoop? Slope? Began with an S.

Philip hadn't read these books either. We both agreed that there was one very excellent book that we had read aeons ago called – *The Power and the Glory*? *The Shame and the Pity*? Anyway, it was the Something and the Something. But the What and the What? Oh well somebody at *The Observer* must be able to find that out, I said. (An American professor of English literature, to whom I related this story, was scandalized: 'You mean a reviewer of Philip Toynbee's stature didn't have any reference books in his house?' That wouldn't be his form, I explained. He did have tons of books but not what one might call reference books.)

What about Faulkner's attitude to race discrimination? asked Philip. Very murky and convoluted, I said. He doubtless had that white Southern mix of nostalgia for the past and guilt about the present, but he never spoke out for black liberation. On the contrary. I had read in a rare interview (for Faulkner was reclusive, and avoided the press) that should the Black Power movement get out of hand, he would feel bound to take up arms against it as a Mississippi white.

I had spent some hours with the great man, I told Philip, in 1952 when I was part of a White Women's delegation touring Mississippi to gain support for Willie McGee, a black man sentenced to death for raping a white woman; all the evidence pointed to the fact she was McGee's willing, in fact insistent, mistress for years, and that only when her husband found out about the affair did she accuse McGee of rape. Faulkner had been fascinated by this circumstance, compounded of his favourite themes; sex, race, and violence. As he rambled on, I took notes of his conversation and that evening composed it into a press release for the Willie McGee defense. Next day, I went back to see Faulkner and asked him to OK the release. He did so, saying however: 'I think they should BOTH be destroyed.' 'Oh don't let's put that,' said I, and dashed to my car with the signed statement.

Philip was interested in all this, but the clock was ticking away. Ten-thirty – eleven . . . He disappeared, and emerged shortly before twelve having completed the task.

The next morning we rushed to get the Sunday papers – to me, a recurrent mystery that these could have been printed in London and delivered in deepest Monmouthshire within less than twenty-four hours.

The Sunday Times obit writer had it all correct: he plodded on describing Faulkner's major work about Yoknapatawpha County, and the Snopes family who dwelled therein. Yet Philip's was so much more interesting – marvellously well written, with many a flash-back to our early morning conversation of the day before.

'I must confess that I have never been quite at my ease with Faulkner's books,' Philip wrote (well – no wonder, as he had never actually read most of them). 'In all except the marvellous and inimitable *The Sound and the Fury* I had a recurring sense of strain and artifice . . .'

My contribution was paraphrased as follows: 'It has also been said by some critics who judge writers mainly by their social and political attitudes that Faulkner was ambiguous in his whole treatment of race in the Southern States. He issued no fighting proclamations against white oppression . . . But I believe that this, too, is a mistaken criticism.'

I was proud and pleased to be cast as 'some critics'. It was

my moment of sound, fury, power, glory – although I
thought it was a shame and a pity that Philip hadn't included
the McGee case.

This incident was by no means characteristic of Philip's
general attitude to literary criticism; on the contrary, he took
pride in his self-imposed discipline, unusual in reviewers, of
reading a book from cover to cover before starting to write his
review. Not, for him, the hack writer's propensity to extrapo-
late from the jacket blurb, then to skim quickly through the
book in search of a few quotable bits to praise or blame.

He was on the whole generous to the writers he reviewed,
sensing no doubt the pains suffered – akin to his own – in
preparing a book for publication, and then casting it into the
uncertain seas, to sink or swim – or be done to death by sharks.

An example of this generosity: I was staying at Cob Cottage
in 1959, shortly after Philip had reviewed *Beloved Infidel* by
Sheilah Graham. This book had been the target of furious
invective in English reviews, editorials, front-page news
stories, because of the author's revelation of how she had
cleverly managed to claw her way up from an East End
orphanage into English high society, eventual presentation at
court, subsequent success in Hollywood and marriage to F.
Scott Fitzgerald.

Alone amongst the scavengers of this lurid tale of duplicity
and intrigue, Philip had given it a favourable review; he rather
admired Sheilah Graham's tenacity, her successful hoodwink-
ing of aristocratic dupes – a super-tease on the Upper Classes,
as he saw it.

My Uncle Jack Mitford, himself a rather disreputable character, had been largely instrumental in furthering Sheilah
Graham's ambitions. One of her dreams was to become a
member of the International Sportsmen's Club in Grosvenor
House, and it was Uncle Jack, a founder of the club, who
arranged this.

Philip asked me about the club: what were its great attractions? Not manifold, I answered. It was a sort of glorified YMCA, with a skating rink, gymnasium, swimming bath and a semi-posh restaurant, much frequented by Mitford aunts and uncles who often took us to lunch there when we were children.

That day, Philip had a letter from Sheilah Graham brimming over with gratitude for his kind review; much to our amusement, it was written on the letterhead of the International Sportsmen's Club.

CHAPTER 9

The Fearful Choice

The Fearful Choice, published by Gollancz in 1958 and the following year by Wayne University Press in Detroit, was Philip's compilation of answers to a letter he had circulated in 1957 to seventy-five public figures in England. Re-read in 1982, year of world-wide demonstrations against nuclear weaponry, this quarter-of-a-century-old discussion sounds a surprisingly contemporary note. In the respondents' letters all the viewpoints and pro/con arguments that we hear today are represented. These range from E. M. Forster's affecting comment, 'There was a baby in our Christmas gathering up in the Midlands, and the contrast between the love it expected and received and the cruelty maturing for it outside was at moments unbearable', to Kingsley Amis's view that, 'given the chance of a savage Russian occupation . . . I'm prepared to see us going on as we are, horrible as that is.' A. J. P. Taylor comes down for unilateral nuclear disarmament: 'the bombs and bases are not here for our sake, but solely because the Americans can't fire the stuff from their own soil'; while most liberals – MP's, clergymen, writers – hover anxiously betwixt and between, as was and is their wont, then and today.

When this book arrived in the mail I thought it riveting. To put it in context: In the late 1950s, the United States was still very much in thrall to what is called in a sort of historical shorthand 'McCarthyism'. Senator McCarthy had died but his spirit lived on. 'The 'Peace Movement', such as it was, and its various offspring – 'Ban the Bomb', 'Women Strike for Peace', etc – consisted of a few stout, embattled left-wingers subject to constant harassment by the FBI and numerous witch-hunting committees.

That *The Fearful Choice* could be published at all in America (albeit by an obscure University Press) seemed, in those days, something of a breakthrough. I determined to review it, but where? There were few choices. I had yet to publish my first book, and had no entree to magazines, so I settled for the *Peoples World*, West Coast counterpart of the *Daily Worker*.

Choosing what I thought was an arresting passage in *The Fearful Choice*, I began my review:

> 'For all I know it is within the providence of God that the human race should destroy itself in this manner. There is no evidence that the human race is to last forever and plenty in Scripture to the contrary effect . . . Christ in His Crucifixion showed us how to suffer creatively . . .'
> Thus writes the wicked old Archbishop of Canterbury.

A month later I had a letter from Philip:

> A few days ago I got a batch of photostated reviews from Wayne University Press and was ploughing rather drearily through them when I suddenly came on one which began, expectedly enough, with a quote from the Archbishop. Imagine my amazement to see this followed by the sentence, 'Thus writes the wicked old Archbishop of Canterbury . . .' Not *at all* the tone of others which, even when mildly favourable, were dreary to a degree. So I looked to see who wrote it, and all became clear.

In his letter to the seventy-five notables, which serves as introduction to *The Fearful Choice*, Philip wrote that, 'Possibilities which are much spoken of are often very little apprehended, and there are few people in England who have really contemplated nuclear warfare.' Drawing a vivid picture of pulverization, vast numbers killed, maimed, condemned to a slow death by radiation, he posed a 'simple test for deciding whether or not we have truly contemplated the reality' of such a war:

> Have we decided how we are to kill the other members of our household in the event of our being less injured than they are? . . . Over most of the country there will probably be a chaos of people dying in isolation from each other, and in great agony . . . Much needless anguish can be avoided if we are at least prepared with our methods of euthanasia.

Dwight MacDonald once remarked to Abbie Hoffman, intrepid anti-Establishment warrior and organizer of the Yippies in the 1960s, 'What ever possessed you people? The notion of acting out your ideas defies the intellectual tradition.' This observation applies perfectly to Philip who resolutely, in fact ruthlessly, put his ideas into practice, often with disconcerting and alarming results, as I was to discover when the Toynbees and their children came to stay at Inch Kenneth, my mother's remote island in the Inner Hebrides, shortly after publication of *The Fearful Choice*.

It was in many ways an idyllic holiday. To my pleased surprise (for I had been slightly apprehensive about inviting these possibly incompatible guests) my mother liked the Toynbees, although she was mildly critical of Sally for failing to look after Philip's clothes which were in truth somewhat disreputable; his one tweed jacket was falling apart, the elbows nothing but gaping holes. 'You'd think Sally could darn that for him,' said my mother.

For once the Scottish weather behaved with unaccustomed benignness. Redheaded, freckle-faced Jason aged six ('The very picture of Huckleberry Finn', as Philip said) and four-year-old Lucy, a rare beauty, went scrambling about the rocks and beaches with their contemporaries, the children of the McGillivrays, my mother's boatman and his wife, the only other inhabitants of Inch Kenneth. Philip remarked that children of that age are like part of the flora and fauna of the countryside – 'the pathos of being shorter than a gooseberry bush!' He daily braved the freezing North Atlantic for a swim, thus earning my mother's approbation: 'I *do* like to see young men getting out in the lovely air and sea', she said of Philip, then in his mid-forties.

Together Philip and Bob roamed the isle – 'One hundred acres of arable land', as Bob told him, but not much of a walk; more of a stroll through a mile or so of grass interspersed with sheep droppings and cow-pats. Philip, having stepped into one of these to the detriment of his already-done-for shoes, told me with his incomparable chuckle: 'Bob said, "When Decca and I take over this island, we'll have all those turds swept away." He doesn't realize they are like minted gold, worth the earth – they *are* the earth in fact.' Bob, of course, was fully aware of this ecological fact, but enjoyed playing up to Philip in the part of an innocent urban American. Thereafter Philip dubbed Bob 'the Young Laird of Inch Kenneth'.

For the grown-ups, every evening at 6 p.m. was the hallowed moment for the BBC news, our one link with the outside world – the newspapers were often a day late in their progression by land and sea to Inch Kenneth.

'Russians resume nuclear testing' was the major import of one such broadcast. The next morning the Toynbees, grave-faced and a bit embarrassed, broached to me the possibility of going to Tobermory for the day. Could I ask my mother if she would arrange this? I was amazed: nothing could be more inconvenient than an impromptu trip to Tobermory. It meant stirring forth McGillivray, who would have to transport them across the sea to Mull, and thence in my mother's ancient Morris Minor, kept pristine in a shed on the opposite shore, over twelve miles of winding roads to Tobermory, and later in the day, repeat the exercise in the other direction. Why on earth, I asked? They couldn't explain the reason, they said. The pained urgency of their expressions drove me to make this unprecedented request; my mother acceded.

The Toynbees returned late, dishevelled and flustered, bearing with them an enormous bottle containing one thousand aspirins. Later, a sheepish Philip explained. They had inadvertently left home without the euthanasia medicine for the children. They had hoped to get some in Tobermory – 'Oh *honestly*, what a preposterous idea', I remonstrated. Tobermory – the least likely place in the world to be dishing out suicide pills. Aspirins? To get four-year-old Lucy to choke down two of them if needed for a sore throat would take some doing. The forced feeding of a killing dose – at least a hundred – might be almost worse, from her point of view, than the dire consequences of nuclear war . . .

And what of Sally? After all, they were her children too. She told me later that she hadn't wanted to go to Tobermory in search of the pills: 'I was angry, appalled at the whole idea.' Philip had been accumulating lethal doses for over a year:

> He had begged and borrowed different kinds of sleeping pills from a few friends in 1956–7, when many considered a nuclear holocaust to be imminent. The thought that a particular bottle in our medicine cabinet contained the dose required to dispose of our children horrified me. The pills were selected with an eye to the colour of their coatings so the children wouldn't be alarmed, or guess what they were – the macabre intent being that they should resemble Smarties!

But in this matter, as in many another in the course of their long life together, Sally was buffeted into acquiescence by the very force of Philip's passionate advocacy.

There is a footnote to Philip's commitment to euthanasia. A few years later the Toynbees came back to Inch Kenneth. My mother had died, so this time the Young Laird and I were the hosts. With the help of the McGillivrays we put on a banquet (as we grandly announced it on the invitations) for neighbouring islanders. Some thirty people, grown-ups and children, showed up for this event – a tremendous feast of salmon, hams, assorted puddings and cakes, plus many a 'wee dram' as the Scots call large draughts of whisky. To accommodate uncertain tides the 'banquet' was called for 2 p.m. We had an essay contest for the children judged by Philip; we danced the Highland Fling in the drawing-room until, if not dawn, its Highland equivalent – about 8 p.m., when the last guests drifted off into their boats.

Soon McGillivray came to announce that some holiday yachters had arrived at our safe harbour wanting milk and fresh water, requests routinely honoured by denizens of the Hebrides. Philip, who had been downing wee drams before, during and after the banquet, as indeed I had, insisted that we should offer hospitality, so we staggered forth into the twilight to meet the yachters at the pier.

Even in my dram-filled state I noted the incongruity: there was I, still in my banquet garb (what was then called a cocktail dress), and there were the yachters, a pleasant-faced couple with their nine-year-old son all in their foul-weather togs, stout windbreakers and practical jeans. The yachters were murmuring understated thanks; Philip was exuberantly waving them towards the house, inviting them for a wee dram of their choice.

They accepted a glass of sherry. Philip then sprang on them:

'If you wanted to kill your children, how would you go about it?' To which the wife answered, 'Well – I think that would depend on the *age* of the child,' which I thought on target. About now the nine-year-old, a polite little boy who hadn't spoken until then, said rather urgently, 'Mummy, don't you think it's time we got back to the boat?'

CHAPTER 10

Barn House Community

Thinking back, it seems to me that the various transforma-
tions of Barn House were indicators of Philip's strong and
sweeping moods, the all-out tug of war between God and
Mammon, as he perceived it, that dominated his later years.

When Bob and I first went to stay with the Toynbees in
Barn House in the early sixties, it was a comfortably sloppy
dwelling, with a pretty exterior, a flourishing vegetable garden tended by Sally, a large apple orchard. The house was
roomy enough to accommodate their three children and a few
guests. The sole bathroom was a-clutter with tennis shoes,
toys, several towels in various stages of use, the twin lavatory
paper as of old. Philip, leading us through, said that when
David Astor had come to stay and was shown this facility he
asked, 'Oh – is this *my* bathroom?'

We returned a few years later to witness Transformation
Number One. The tiny sitting room in which we huddled
round a coal fire, the children strewn about the floor because
there were never enough chairs, had been extended and somewhat incongruously refurbished with fitted wall-to-wall
carpeting. Philip's own quarters now boasted a lovely huge
modern bathroom done up in gold and white – to which

guests, however, were not admitted: for us, it was the un-changed David Astor bathroom. A brand-new central heating plant had been installed. As in his maze-building days, Philip was at work on extraordinary, unlikely landscaping projects; he had created a mini-Xanadu waterfall that cascaded endlessly into a swimming pool in which the children, now almost grown-up, disported themselves. We older folk sat in com-fortable garden furniture round the edges downing draughts of Pimm's Cup. In *Part of a Journey*, Philip writes that his 'water garden' as he called it took two years of unremitting hard labour to create. Some were critical of the end result: 'Awful bits of plastic bobbing about', said Anne, and Josephine, 'the wrinkled polythene lining of the pond, like dust-bin liner material, held down by stones round the edge of the pond, protruded above the level of the surface giving it an unnatural and rather tatty appearance.' Polly said *she* never got any Pimm's Cup. I, then, must have seen it all through the rose-coloured specs of its creator; to me, it was a dazzling achievement.

As for Transformation Number Two, we heard rumours of it for some time before we actually saw and experienced it. Philip was turning his home into a Commune, we were told, in which an Alternative Lifestyle would exemplify the true brotherhood of man; simplicity, the city dweller's dream of a return to the soil, were to be put into practice. Mammon was now banished (or alleged to be; actually he was forever lurking in the wings) and pure selflessness was the order of the day. Bob and I elected to put up at a nearby pub, from which we emerged at suitable times to observe all this high-minded togetherness in action. As usual, Philip was the energetic prime mover; Sally, ever supportive, trailed rather unhappily in his wake.

Or so it seemed to me at the time. But Sally now maintains that she opposed the Commune from the beginning; Philip, she says, was by nature and temperament the most unsuitable candidate imaginable for the Communal life. For years, she had acted as buffer between him and the outside world. 'He hated seeing anyone arrive unexpectedly, or unannounced,' she said. 'If the phone rang, I'd always answer and find out who was calling so Philip could decide if he wanted to talk to them. Or if somebody knocked at the door, he'd hide upstairs until I found out who it was. He couldn't bear any random invasion of his privacy.' At first, Sally hoped and believed that the Commune scheme was just talk: 'My original thought was that he'd never do it. But the plans were firmed up, and he took steps to implement them.'

Barn House now was a scene of devastation. Under the direction of an Alternative Architect found by Philip through an advertisement he had spotted in *Alternative Society*, Sally's commodious kitchen with all its conveniences (a product of Transformation Number One) had been converted into a sort of scullery for the preparation of natural food, vegetables and the like. The environmentally offensive central heating had been taken out. The elegant staircase had been demolished and the hall divided into ugly little cubicles to house the inflow of Communards and their children. Yet devoted though he was to the concept and to its execution, Philip absolutely saw the joke of it all – including the repulsive 'Alternative' jargon he now adopted – which for me was the redeeming feature that caused me to return time and again to this odd milieu. I went there quite often; sometimes with Bob, sometimes with Anne, or Ben Nicolson, and on one memorable occasion with Bob, my daughter Dinky and her children.

A marvellous travelling companion on these safaris to Toynbeeland was Ben Nicolson, for thirty years Philip's best friend.

I had heard of Ben Nicolson all my life, as a son of the strange union of Harold Nicolson and Vita Sackville-West, but met him only late in life as an occasional fellow-guest at the Toynbees. I found him a wonderfully comic – yet profound –

character. His face! I can almost recreate it by standing in front of a looking-glass and energetically pulling the cheeks downwards with both hands. He had the elongated monk's face of a medieval painting, combining a certain asceticism with a hint of appreciation of such carnal pleasures as good food and wine.

He was a delightful ally in my sometimes losing, often winning, tussles with Philip about God and Mammon; Ben was clearly on Mammon's side, if a trifle out of touch with the latter's modern ways. Once, at a large luncheon in one of those absurd, overpriced castles-turned-restaurants that abound in the English countryside, somebody said that she had got to go to the dentist.

'The dentist,' said Ben lugubriously. 'Such *torture*, specially when he starts *drilling*'; and he pumped his foot up and down in demonstration.

'But Ben,' we all said, 'those foot drills were discontinued shortly after the First World War.'

'Oh,' said Ben, his long face growing longer, 'No wonder he can *always* fit me in for an appointment, no matter how *late* I ring up.'

'And I suppose your doctor regularly leeches you,' observed Philip.

Perhaps at this point it would be only fair to give Philip's view of one of these visits, contained in his article for the *Radio Times* of 1977. He wrote:

> 'But Bim is *bliss!*' said Decca.
> Bim, a bearded young man in sweater and jeans, went even redder in the face; but did his best to keep his end up.
> 'What did you say your next book is about?'
> 'Unrequited love!' moaned Decca, looking at him with languishing, beautiful but short-sighted eyes behind her specs.
> Bim gave a rough guffaw of defeat; and the party had begun. On Decca's terms, of course.
> The scene was an agricultural commune to which I am attached, and of which Bim Mason, aged 21, has been a member since its beginning nearly three years ago. I had been

playing a favourite game of mine, and one which I have
constantly enjoyed during the forty years which have passed
since Decca Mitford and I first met in a little flat between the
warehouses of Rotherhithe. The game is to get her into a set of
human circumstances which seems as unsuitable as possible to
her character, manner, personal history and disposition. Our
commune is everything which Decca is not – concerned with
the land and outdoor work; almost entirely indifferent to
material comforts; deeply preoccupied with self-awareness,
growth and the conscious development of human relations;
inclined towards religious beliefs of one sort or another. These
young friends of mine are light-hearted people; but they are
not frivolous.

Except for Bim, an extremely likable, intelligent and hard-
working lad, I have little recollection of the Communards. In
any event the cast of characters was constantly changing as
these Alternative People came and, having scant experience of
or stomach for the rigours of farming life, soon departed.
Disaffected urban school teachers, university students bent on
Finding Themselves – flotsam and jetsam of English society.

I would greet them in passing after stepping out of my sleek
hotel into the ever-increasing squalor of Barn House, and
observe their ill-behaved children, their sad-faced wives going
very slowly about their chores for which they clearly had little
enthusiasm.

As for Philip: Sally told me later, with her characteristic lack
of bitterness, that he never relinquished *his* comfortable quarters – while she was consigned to one of the cubicles. Clara,
their youngest and the only one still living at home, then going
through the torment of adolescence, was never consulted in
any way about these drastic changes of circumstances.

I knew little of the spiritual aspects of the Commune until
much later, when I read *Part of a Journey*. However, as a very
occasional visitor, I did notice that it took little persuasion to
lure the Toynbees from the Commune to greener pastures in
the form of long, luxurious lunches in the Crown, an excellent

nearby pub. 'Ready for a spot of quail on toast, Philip?' I'd ask, and Philip, looking anxiously round to make sure the Communards were not in earshot, would quickly concur. Fingers to lips, shushing each other, Ben, Sally, Philip and I would nip swiftly to the getaway car, Philip giving a cheery wave to any Communard in sight: 'Just fetching some supplies from the village.'

After one of these excursions I sent him a bread-and-butter letter in verse, to the tune of 'In Dublin's Fair City':

> In Brockweir's fair city
> Where the Toynbees sat pretty
> They decided to forgo the comforts of life
> With no central heating
> And a minimum of eating
> Crying 'Communes! Alternatives! Alive, alive-oh.'

> An alternative architect
> Who came out to inspect
> Said 'take out the dishwasher, gas pipes and stove,
> If you think you might freeze
> Just cut down some trees'
> Crying, 'Communes! Alternatives! Alive, alive-oh.'

> As a way to cut down bills
> They were soon into windmills
> But the wind from the willows refused to be budged;
> So the Toynbees in despair
> To the Crown went for jugged hare
> Crying 'Don't tell the Commune, alive, alive-oh'

> From sun-up to sun-down
> When friends come from London
> The pleasures of life are resumed in full force;
> Like escapers from gaol
> They sneak out for quail
> Crying 'Don't tell the Commune, alive, alive-oh.'

> When Ben came with Decca
> They found it a mecca
> Of drinking and eating and lounging about,

And blow-outs at the Crown
So they went back to town
Crying 'We'll tell Lord Longford, alive, alive-oh.'

I soon had Philip's answer: 'We all loved your brave little
whistle in the dark, and have stuck it up in most honoured
space on community notice-board. But truth will out, so I'm
cruelly sending you a teeny morsel of truth in return. Pass on
to Ben some time. It was heavenly having you and Ben here.
Come again soon when conditions are rougher and we can
give you a *real* taste of community life.'

There followed an Auden-esque ballad:

It's Christmas night in the Year of our Lord
Nineteen-Eighty-Four
And the snow is piling thick and fast
Against the Barn House door.

Now the windmills up on top of the roof
Are merrily whirling round,
And all the bulbs are blazing bright
To the wood-stove's merry sound.

An organically-fattened turkey roasts
Around his organical stuffing
And the solar-heated oven gives off
A yuletide huffing and puffing.

Oh Bim and Sal and Fiona raise
Their glasses of gooseberry wine
And Philip, Dave and Clara exclaim:-
'*Does'nt* it taste divine!'

Lichen and Maya are gaily pulling
A little alternative cart,
And even the dogs have learnt to blow
A sweet alternative fart.

But suddenly over the butter-bean beds
Two wretched creatures appear:

The seem to be nothing but rags and bones
As they crawl and mutter and peer.

And now through the kitchen window gape
The hollow cheeks and eyes
Of a 'thing' that was once a man, perhaps,
And the wreck of a 'woman', who cries:-

'Oh won't you let us inside, my loves,
For we are Decca and Ben:
We've crawled all the way from London Town,
From our blacked-out Mayfair den.

'O you were right and we were wrong,'
The starving authoress whines.
'Yes, we were wrong and you were right'
Her squalid companion opines.

'O I was a system art-editor!'
'And I was as straight as could be!'
'But now that we've seen how right you were
Won't you give us a cup of tea?

'For there's no more quail at The Crown, my dears;
And there's no more scotch at the Ritz.
Titians are selling at sixpence a piece
And our publisher's out of his wits.'

Now David, Sally, Philip and Bim,
Lichen and Clara too,
Agree with Fiona and Maya who say,
'To our principles we must be true.

"Peace and Love" was ever our cry,
So when we've finished our dinners
Instead of saving the swill for the pigs
We'll throw it to those poor sinners.'

'Oh *thank* you, sirs!' cry Ben and Decca,
'And thank you, ladies, too!
We'll bless the Barn House Community
Though we freeze black and blue.

Bless you, all our alternative chums,
For we who had mocked you so
Have found our counter-culture at last
Out in the communal snow.'

I did pass it on to Ben, who answered:

I add my own little clerihew:

> The trouble about Decca
> Is that she is a born wrecker.
> When confronted by the alternative society
> She consumes quails to the point of satiety.

How delicious your exchange of correspondence with Philip! This is a thing to keep. And in 2074 the professor of twentieth-century literature at Hong Kong will give it a learned footnote.

Sally had her own escape hatch in the form of a one-day-a-week job as a volunteer in the Monmouth Citizen's Advice Centre, one of those crisis centres to which people in various kinds of trouble can apply for help. Once, when Bob and I were at the Commune, I got the telephone number from Philip, and rang up there on Sally's day in the office. Assuming a sort of pidgin French, I said: "Allo, 'allo, ees zees zee advice bureau? Alors, je suis Algérienne. I am an Algerian. I 'ave two 'usband, and I want a room vis one bed for my two men.' Sally answered that Monmouth is a rather conservative town, and it might be difficult to make this arrangement. 'But je suis Mormon, my religion eet ess Mormon,' I pleaded. 'I must 'ave my two men in von bed.' In that case, said Sally, perhaps she could find a Mormon group in Monmouth who could help? (Likely story, thought I!) 'Mormon c'est ma religion but I do not vant zee Mormon group,' I said. 'Mais je understand qu'il y a un Monsieur Toynbee qui 'ave a very fine Commune. . . ' 'DECCA, I knew it was you all along!' said Sally crossly. (Philip, of course, was standing close enough to hear every word, shaking with silent laughter. We all agreed afterwards that Sally, if she had thought back to American history, would have realized the fraudulence of my alleged predicament: Mormon *men* had multiple *wives*, not the other way round.)

When Sally came home she told us that later that day a genuine 'crisis' case had rung up: a man with a heavy foreign accent. She had said 'Bob! I *know* that's you.' In such minor amusements did we while away the time at the Commune.

As time went on Philip, committed as ever to putting his ideas into practice, promulgated new rules. Total self-sufficiency for the Commune was now the goal, and to this end he cut down the apple orchard to provide pasture for a cow – 'takes a year or two for the grass to grow,' he said. 'So don't be expecting milk and cheese for some time.' The Commune, with its ever-changing population, would have to make do without electricity; windmills would supply all energy needs. But (as Sally told me later), 'engineering problems proved too complex and costly, so that toasting forks and scrubbing boards became the order of the day.' When the electric clothes-washing machine was dismantled, the sad-faced wives grew sadder yet. Faced with hand-scrubbing their babies' nappies, some were alleged to have sneaked off into Monmouth to avail themselves of the coin-operated laundromats at relatively vast expense.

My last glimpse of that dread Commune was in the autumn of 1974, when Bob and I went to stay there with Dinky and her two children aged seven and five.

The Commune had turned, predictably, into a horror scene. I particularly remember a moment in which I asked Sally if I could lie down for a bit in the afternoon. She led me into Jason's old bedroom, which happened to be empty. It was freezing cold. Soon Sally came back with an electric blanket, saying as she plugged it in, 'For God's sake don't tell Philip. It consumes electric energy, he doesn't know I've still got it.'

An uneasy feeling of intrigue was in the air. Philip and

Sally seemed to be circling each other, like secret agents of opposing regimes spying out weaknesses. Clara, at the miserable age of sixteen, represented the innocent civilian population caught in the midst of high-level plots she neither understood nor welcomed.

All the jolly jokes were over; there was indeed 'no more quail at the Crown, my dears.' One evening there was a sort of show-down, initiated by Dinky who was far from amused, was in fact appalled by the whole scene, particularly as it affected the 'Communard' mothers of young children and as it was clearly affecting poor Clara.

Somehow the five of us – Philip, Sally, Dink, Bob and I – detached ourselves from the others. There followed one of our rare dead serious conversations with Philip, unrelieved by his usual clowning.

Dinky, American by birth and upbringing, sensible by nature and attuned to socialist principles by inclination, conducted a rigorous and incisive cross-examination. In her forthright fashion, eyes blazing, she questioned every assumption of the Commune, from its alleged egalitarian goals to the exploitation of the nappy-scrubbing mothers to the failure to consider Clara's views. From time to time, Bob and I came in on Dink's side in the discussion. In fact, we took what seems on looking back unforgivable liberties, and virtually turned the conversation into one of those awful 'encounter groups' loved by Philip, loathed by us. Had we somehow fallen prey to the Commune atmosphere of Total Frankness – and this, after a visit of but a few days?

I must have written to Philip to apologize for our dreadful, governessy and (I hoped) untypical behaviour that evening; in any event, his next letter, undated, is headed 'The Broken Nest':

> Not to worry – I mean, not to worry about *us*, anyway. We love you all as much as ever, though I do admit that I *was* a bit

cross when actually under the bombardment. I still think a small part of your and Bob's motive for such vehemence may have been general anti-community sentiment rather than absolutely pure love for one-and-all. But who has driven-snow motives anyway? And as for me, I am really much enjoying present house-hunt; feel the general shake-up may be all for the good in the long run.

The Toynbees, then, had decided to move out, and find other quarters for themselves. Why did they not simply announce to the Communards that (in the words of that excellent song of the 1930s) 'I'm afraid the masquerade is over, And so is love'? But no. This was not the mood of the moment, as far as Philip was concerned. The Commune was left intact, in the increasingly unwilling hands of its Alternative inhabitants.

The new nest, to which the Toynbees moved soon after that atrocious evening, was Woodroyd Cottage, about two miles from the Barn House Commune. Compared to Barn House in pre-Commune days it was a bit of a starling's nest, twigs thrown together higgledy-piggledy, although Sally with her talent for creating comfort had got some areas in order. I only went there once, shortly before the final dissolution of the Commune. Communards would come and go, fetching and delivering things between the two houses. Philip was almost unnaturally cheerful and welcoming on these occasions: 'Oh hallo, hallo, do come in and meet an old friend from America . . . '

Some of Philip's friends were spared the Commune drama. Paddy Leigh Fermor says he was only kept abreast of it by fits and starts, although Philip had outlined the idea during a picnic at Tintern Abbey. 'I had never heard of a worse plan,' said Paddy. 'He appeared to me, all at once, as a figure out of Peacock, determined to put theory into immediate practice, like the Shelley and Byron figures of the novels. Hence the Commune, on the edge of those Peacockian forests where he

lived on the Marches of Wales — and his unresentful abandon-
ment of it for a more restful solitude with Sally.'

The unanswered question in my mind was why this absurd,
pre-doomed experiment? I feared to ask Philip, who was often
in the throes of 'clinical depression', a pit of despair unimaginable to one who has not suffered it. But his daughter
Josephine, who like me and other Toynbee friends and fans
had dipped into the Commune from time to time, offered
some useful clues in what she describes as 'a rather solemn little
analysis':

When the transformation of Barn House was first mooted,
both my father and Sally had become deeply involved in the
ecology movement. The ideology of this movement pulled
together so many different strands of his nature. Its demand for
a passionate political commitment, condemning the exploitation of the starving Third World by the grossly overfed nations
of the West, called on that which had earlier led him into the
Communist Party, and a lifelong socialism. The ecology
movement's prediction of an impending environmental catastrophe, brought about by mankind's blind selfishness, was
seized upon by my father with the fervour of an Old Testament
prophet as a call for a personal preparedness and a public stand,
much as he had taken the Nuclear Disarmament cause to heart.
The pronounced demand for a change to a simpler life-style,
based on honest human labour and co-operation with others,
appealed to his 'virtuous', more austere side. Barn House, and
similar communes around the country, were to be the new
Arks, and there was real agonizing about how, with the
imminent and inevitable breakdown of society, the commune
would receive the starving hordes from the cities.

At the same time their two older children, Jason and Lucy,
had left home, and Barn House seemed large and empty, an
invitation to my father's ever-ready guilt about his patrician
background and his comparative wealth. (He never could take
in that his salary, on which they lived, now whittled away by
inflation, was well under the national average.)

In an act of supreme moral resolution, coated in frenzied
enthusiasm, my father, who had spent much of his life acting

out the extremes of his nature – between indulgence and deprivation, vice and virtue, autocracy and egalitarianism, tragedy and farce, conviviality and seclusion – committed himself and all that he held valuable to the new project.

The personal cost, to himself and his family, was enormous, but he was ruthless in the application of his ideals. Never mind that he was increasingly a recluse by nature, communal living would enable him to slough off his privileges, live out a true egalitarianism, work hard and productively on the land, and become a better man. While earlier passions had been excursions from which he could retreat, this was to involve *all* that was worthwhile in him. Mercifully he held on to his saving gift, and never let go of his writing and reviewing.

The strain of wrenching together his contrary nature proved almost intolerable. When I was there the communal lunches, dominated by bad jokes and false *bonhomie* by my father, were followed by his retreat to bed, and ever longer and blacker depressions. He insisted on defining this depression as physical in origin, consuming vast quantities of tranquillizers and anti-depressants, and eventually seeking out doctors who were willing to prescribe ECT. But I am convinced that he was oppressed by having flung himself into a tunnel from which there seemed no way out.

He soon came to see some members of the commune as layabouts and charlatans, and mimicked and described them with comic brilliance during the short breaks he allowed himself to see old friends and resume his buffoon's guise. But there were also a number of gentle, intelligent, dedicated people whom he respected. Yet it really would not have mattered if they had been angels; the strain lay in the demand he made upon himself in having them there at all. Ironically, it was Sally who, while thinking the idea of a commune a mistake, found it easier to make friends and live together with individual communards.

My father used the commune as a testing ground for his project of self-improvement. The communards' differences from himself, their antagonism to routine, leadership, or organization, served as a measure for his own values. He, who had always alternated between wilful austerity and fits of debauchery, tried to absorb and emulate their values of easy acceptance of themselves and one another, trusting in a slow, organic, too often imperceptible development. His comments on them veered from wondrous admiration for their easy sharing together, lack of competition, and openness to new ideas, to a maddened exasperation that things were not getting done, that they had no sense of purpose, or self-discipline.

After he and Sally and Clara had moved away to Woodroyd he still counted himself as a full working member of the commune. But as most members had come in the pursuit of an ideal, the rub and clash of their various approaches soon focused far more attention upon the ultimate purposes of life, and away from the monotonous exigencies of every-day farming. Simon and Bim still laboured on the land and milked the cows, looking with some scepticism upon the others' increasing emphasis on self-discovery and meditation. My father too, while contributing his share of labour, was by now more interested in spiritual discoveries. Sunday evenings at Barn House, much to Sally's embarrassment, became eclectic religious and ritual occasions, with group meditation, the chanting of 'Om', spontaneous prayers, and processions with candles. The commune consciously resolved that its object was no longer ecological survival, but shared explorations in spiritual growth, and it subsisted, more or less, by some members taking gardening and agricultural odd jobs around the neighbourhood.

An influential figure at this stage was an enthusiastic young New Zealander named Kerry, who was making explorations into the newer radical Christianity of Hans Küng, and the mingling of Zen Buddhism and Christianity of Thomas Merton. He and my father eagerly exchanged books and ideas, and it was he and some members of more traditional Christian background who discovered the beautiful Anglican convent at Tymawr, which holds services open to the public on Sundays. They introduced my father to the nuns. It was here that he was to find his spiritual home and a life of deep religious involvement, that finally enabled him to let go of the mental constructs which had tied him so painfully to the commune.

Sally, to whom I sent my account of the Commune, disagrees with much of it. 'I realize that it has been difficult to decide how far to bend the truth for the sake of a laugh,' she wrote. 'Most of my comments/corrections apply to those areas of Philip's life which were either unfamiliar or alien to you (or both).' Her strictures follow:

> It is incorrect to say that the 'cast of characters was always changing'. The minor parts, taken by prospective members & visitors, were mutable, but the principals remained fairly constant.
>
> It is neither fair nor accurate to say that the majority represented the 'flotsam & jetsam of society'. With very few exceptions, they were people who wished to create for themselves a better way of life through sharing work, beliefs & responsibilities. Some had come from reasonably comfortable circumstances. Two had university degrees and most had had some kind of gainful employment. They all shared the desire to put their high-minded principles into practice.
>
> To my knowledge, there was only one 'sad-faced' wife whose two children, I agree, were ill-behaved. The others were enthusiastic, positive in attitude though perhaps somewhat starry-eyed about the long-term survival of the community. There were very few who came along for the ride, and they were soon weeded out.

However, Sally's benign retrospective view of the denizens of the Barn House Commune is sharply at variance with Philip's own version. As Marina Warner writes in her review of *Part of a Journey*:

> Woven into the diary is the fascinating, funny, appalling tale of the commune to which Philip Toynbee gave his house. This community, intended to be self-supporting and spiritual, declines into a 'crash pad' for freaks until Philip Toynbee decides he must close it and reclaim his house. He agonizes about the ethics of this, but he also draws the Barn House's exploiters with sharp wit.

Philip's descriptions of crumbling relationships with those Alternative People and the final breakup of the Commune are among the best and most revealing passages in the book: a strange, incompatible, potentially combustible mixture of high purpose and high comedy, hallmark of so much of his life and writing.

The Commune's printed prospectus (composed in August 1977 with 'a long bargaining over words and phrases', as Philip wrote – and as I can well imagine) forecasts the shape of things to come.

First off, says the prospectus, the people who came to live in Barn House were

> United by their wish to experience community living and by their common interests in organic gardening and farming.
> But over the years there has been a gradual, and quite unplanned shift of emphasis in the attitudes of most members towards the deeper purposes.

There follows a lengthy paean to a shared life, a love capable of crossing all boundaries, entering into true oneness with each other, a higher power of love, discovering the true Self within, strengthening love, joy and spiritual understanding, a viable and closely-knit family for future growth, etc.

Could Philip have collaborated in – or even 'bargained' over – this sort of prose? Perhaps, for in the middle of this long document is the cannily inserted suggestion that 'two days a week, after breakfasting at the same time, we all work together on our own land or inside the buildings.'

Two days out of seven may seem a short work-week to the average farmer, but the explanation follows; 'In addition to these common activities we also pursue our individual paths, which currently include pottery, puppetry, music, drama, herbal medicine, yoga, tai-chi and private meditation.'

Well – quite so. Three months later (16 November) Philip writes that:

Enthusiasm continues to wane. Lip service is still paid to work as prayer, the holy soil, etc., but meditation, yoga, zikr, even astrology, now take up much time and energy. A threat of angelism here?

And in early 1978 (6 March):

This insistence on 'doing one's own thing' can be simply a form of selfishness . . . Mary, for example, of whom Sally and I are both extremely fond, is going off for her third meditation course next week just at the time when intensive work on the land must be underway.

(14 March):

Simon tells us that there is no longer any enthusiasm for getting the vegetables sown or planted – as indeed I'd guessed from the state of the fields.

Sometimes Philip managed to cajole an unwilling Communard into working alongside. On one such occasion, he and his mate Simon were high on a scaffolding, painting the outside of the house.

Suddenly we heard frightful screams from down the hill. I thought it might be one of the Williams's peacocks; but Simon was so certain it was human that we climbed down quickly and ran into the wood. There we found Phil, looking indeed like a woodland creature, but also a little abashed by our arrival . . . Simon pulled at my sleeve and suggested we get back to our work.

Once out of Phil's earshot I asked Simon what on earth was happening. 'It's only Phil's primal scream therapy,' he said; and when I broke into howls of primal laughter he laughed as well – but a little reluctantly.

Philip adds that it was a miracle that none of the neighbours heard the primal screams, which were quickly resumed after he and Simon left: 'I suspect that primal screamers are too preoccupied with themselves to be much concerned with their neighbours.'

Phil, it develops, had more tricks up his sleeve than the primal scream. A subsequent diary entry:

> As I was starting the fearsome task of cleaning out the big front flower bed at Barn House Phil came up and offered me a whetstone for my hook. Then he stood watching me work, with the full intensity of his shaggy earnestness. I gestured, as if whimsically, at a particularly tall clump of dock and thistle; and Phil thought this over for some time before saying, 'If you mean you want me to do some *work*, Philip, I'm afraid I can't because I'm just going up to meditate with Rose.'
>
> Later, refreshed, I suppose, by his meditation, he appeared again and delivered a little homily to me as I sweated away with hook and stick . . . Hilarious, looked at in one way . . . I realized Phil will *never* do any work here . . . I thanked him quietly for his advice.

If written as satire (which they are, in part) some of Philip's diary entries about the Commune could be taken as progeny of a felicitous union between *Cold Comfort Farm*, Stella Gibbons's 1932 classic parody of the then fashionable earthy school of English writing, and *The Serial* in which Cyra McFadden chronicles the laid-back activities, from TM to Meaningful Interaction, of the with-it generation of the 1970s in Marin County, California.

> There was a very ugly scene at BH. I'd gone over to start the huge task of clearing up the garden, having begged them to do a little of this themselves. But not only had nothing been done; they were lying and lazing about in the ruined garden; soul music from the open window; one very pregnant girl sitting naked on the edge of the swimming pool in full view of the road. What's more half the people there were strangers. A crash pad, in fact, just as Mary had predicted.
>
> I delivered a violent harangue, to which nobody spoke a

single word in answer. It was Them and Us with a vengeance now; the sweet freaks and children of nature up against the angry proprietor whose only thought was to drive them all away and sell the empty house for a fat sum. A melancholy change. Or, as some would say, no change at all, but simply the true situation no longer disguised by kindly pretences from both sides.

A monstrous incubus now appeared in the shape of a young man called John, who arrived unexpectedly during a Barn House Sunday communion: 'a rather mysterious, bearded presence' who 'sat impassively through all our goings-on.'

John, it seems, was not impassive for long. He turned out to be a crusading fundamentalist and revivalist Christian, 'an impressive, infuriating, deeply worrying young man' who had 'a galvanic and confusing effect on the whole community.' One by one the Communards fell under his spell, his 'all-too-charismatic presence' creating

> a state of rather hectic spiritual excitement . . . the point they were all now agreed on was that John's arrival had made them aware of how much BH meant to them; they had never felt so confident in the community's spiritual future as they did now; *this* was the regeneration we had all been waiting and hoping for.

Sally later told me of the ultimate fate of John, whom she described as 'very persuasive, from a titled family, a religious fanatic who thought he had a hotline to God.' It seems that John and a friend, engaged in an act of exorcism which involved thrashing a young woman possessed of the Devil, inadvertently killed her, for which John received a five-year prison sentence. 'Philip read about this at the time,' she said. 'He was furious that the judge gave only five years. He never knew it was "John" who did it until the following year.'

Soon after John's regenerative visit to Barn House, Mammon comes to the rescue (at least that is the way I interpret the final outcome; Philip might have seen it differently).

> I felt basely materialistic when I reminded them of the present economic situation: no money in the kitty; the pick-up a wreck; the fields still a mess; the house itself in desperate need of renovation.
> In the end they took our decision wonderfully well, as we should have known they would.

Philip, at last, getting tough with these parasitic scroungers, got tougher yet. In a subsequent entry he records 'continued ill-feeling, alas, with the remnants of the community'. Informed that 'two of the communards were just going off on yet another meditation course' he said:

> 'No, they can bloody well stay and do some work or bugger off for good.' 'OK, *Landlord!*' said Dave; and stabbed me to the heart, as he intended. (But I pulled his stiletto out pretty smartly as I walked back fuming through the woods.)

Ben Nicolson must have spoken for all of us in his letter to Philip about the final expulsion of the communal remnants:

> Ben was delighted, of course, to hear that we've now definitely decided to bring the community to an end [Philip wrote]. Like nearly all our old friends, he always thought the whole project quite insane; and now he has vigorously encouraged us 'to send the whole lot packing; sell the house; and come to Sicily with me next summer for a proper holiday.'

CHAPTER 11

St Philip

My first real whiff of Philip's unexpected turn to religion came in 1976, when I was away from home and Bob telephoned to read out a letter from Philip. 'Are you sitting down?' said Bob. 'Get this: He writes, "I have decided to become a nun." ' (I am sorry to say that I wrote back saying 'How marvellous that you have decided to become a nun. But I hope you don't get in the habit of it.')

There had, however, been earlier indications of a more public nature. In the late 1960s Robert Kee was doing a series of interviews in what BBC calls the 'God Slot', which had traditionally been filled by clergy of various faiths expounding their views. Robert Kee's series, entitled 'Looking for an Answer', was a departure from this format. He told me:

By that time it was considered OK to get away from organized religion and explore unorthodox ideas, especially of former agnostics – people like Antonia Fraser.

Philip and I had had long discussions about his growing belief in a Deity, so I asked him to come on the programme. His performance came as a great surprise to many of his friends; at one point, he said something like 'Well, old boy, don't *you* sometimes feel like getting down on the old hunkers

and gazing up at Heaven?' Later in the programme he shook his
fist at God – which must have startled some of the viewers. Yet
in a way, this gesture was the essence of his conversion, of his
attitude to God.'

Philip's religious conversion must be, by any reckoning,
one of the oddest – and most unlikely – in ecumenical history.
As a young man, he was stridently anti-church in the old-
fashioned, early twentieth-century sense; for by the time we
were growing up, atheism and agnosticism were pretty
much taken for granted in our circles, and church-baiting was
no longer regarded as daring or amusing. Such issues as
separation of church and state, passionately fought over by
previous generations, would surface from time to time in
perennially earnest journals like the *New Statesman*; but they
were far outside the realm of the political exigencies, as we saw
them, in the 1930s and 1940s.

Not to Philip. According to John Bury, who was stationed
with him in Brussels during the war, he took enormous
pleasure in random and deliberate acts of blasphemy. Bury,
Philip and Brian Urquhart were, I gather, a sort of naughty
and amusing threesome, a wartime comic version of *The
Three Musketeers*.

Philip's bad-boy act of the moment started when he happened to wander into a second-hand shop selling various
trophies, flags, old medals and the like. Amongst this detritus
he spotted two used dog-collars, which he at once seized upon.
He and Bury would venture forth into the town disguised as
clergymen. 'We behaved disgracefully,' said John. 'Every
other word we uttered was an obscenity or a blasphemy.
Once, in a cafe where Philip was being particularly outrageous, a man came up to him and said in all seriousness, "I
say, padre, steady on old boy, steady on!" '

Philip posed in his dog-collar for photographs taken by
Brian Urquhart. One of these shows Philip the Padre leering at
a feelthy postcard, with the caption 'Bugger, Jeepers Creep-

ers!', and in another, taken on the roof of the Brussels Palace Residence in the autumn of 1944, Bury is seen stabbing clergyman Toynbee under the caption, 'Believed to be another of PT's visions of the Disgraceful Surrender and Miserable Fall of the Established Church.'

The gratuitous exercises in blasphemy were, John Bury suggests, a delayed reaction to his mother's adopting of the Roman Catholic faith – a view borne out by Philip's own account in *Part of a Journey*. During his childhood both his parents were agnostics, and he accepted their 'thoughtful scepticism'. When, shortly after his seventeenth birthday, his mother was received into the Church, Philip saw it as a personal betrayal and was deeply hurt and offended. It made him 'passionately and derisively hostile to Christianity, with a particularly sharp resentment against the Roman Church'.

Interestingly, John Bury now interprets the Padre capers as 'scattered clues' to Philip's later religious fervor: 'Perhaps indeed God really was a constant preoccupation throughout his life only submerged for many years, or disguised by an apparent irreligiosity.'

Others, it seems, drew similar conclusions. Frances Partridge gave me her diary entry for 21 September 1964 which affords a vivid, delightful view of Philip as she saw him that day, and a forecast by her husband, Ralph Partridge, of Philip's spiritual trajectory:

> Lunch today at the French pub, with Philip and Terry Kilmartin. I was touched by Philip asking me (the result of the letter I wrote to him about his book [Two Brothers]).
>
> He's enormously charming, wonderfully articulate and surprised one by sudden human and outgoing remarks showing awareness of others. Why surprise? Because there's enough of the rebellious clown about him to rouse an expectation of his being non-human, a sort of 'Spotty John' Strachey.* He's

---

* Friend and painter.

become more wholesome-looking, less outrageous and grubby. I like him in fact very much and do greatly admire his originality and vitality as a writer. Almost at once we got on to the subject of God – and *goodness* how I wished Ralph could have heard his extraordinarily accurate prescience justified! He always declared with absolute conviction that Philip would end up a mystic and probably a believer in God, and he admitted both these today. It was enjoyable to argue with such an intelligent and voluble supporter of religion. Oddly enough his chief justification is the necessity for a first cause. When I brought up the problem of evil, he drew a picture of a well-meaning but *bungling* God, who simply hadn't succeeded in making the universe as good as he would like. But though he declared that he had recently begun to believe in God, he would have nothing to do with J.C. or Christianity. 'And when I've finally proved he does exist, I promise you shall have the scoop for the Observer, Terry! "GOD EXISTS." You'll be able to splash it across the headline.' His affinity with mysticism is almost more suspect. You couldn't treat it like a manic form of insanity, he believes, because mystics are on the whole good and rational people. (I'm not convinced of this). And though he declares he hasn't personally had anything like a mystical experience, he understands enough about it to see that it seems more like knowledge of the universe than anything else. Other reasons for believing in God: That you couldn't believe that 'this salt-cellar' (picking it off the table) could develop into mind, however slowly. (He failed to see that making God the first cause only gave a name to the enigma and pushed it one stage further back. What caused God?) There was a hint too of pragmatism – that if belief in God made you happier it must be true – and comic references to Sally being an alcoholic and having had recourse to the local clergyman, a Mr Sinker, who is trying to explain to her about the Immaculate Conception. She has joined Alcoholics Anonymous though it doesn't seem to have done the trick. Philip has been to gatherings 'on parents's day' and said he was impressed by their good sense and desire to help each other and lack of nonsense. It's ironical that after so many drunken episodes in his own life 'the dog it was that died'.

To his friends, Philip's dramatic philosophical volte-face was a source of puzzlement. Paddy Leigh Fermor writes:

> When asked the year before his death what had prompted his return to religion – it would have seemed out of the question a decade earlier – he said, 'I want to become a better man.' A comic look in his eye hinted that it might sound absurd; but it was precisely what he meant, and though his new allegiance was a comforting anchorage for him, he need never have worried about goodness; and his former unregenerate character will be treasured just as much by his abruptly bereaved old friends.

In a conversation with Robert Kee, Philip summed up his feelings about his 'mysterious relationship with the mind-figure he had in later years been prepared to call God.'

> 'I rail at him,' he said. ' "Lord," I say, "You're a bastard, an absolute bastard. Go away. I hate you." To which He replies very calmly: "Very well, Philip, just as you say. I'll go away then." And I call out after him *desperately*: "Oh, Lord, no! Please! Please come back, Lord . . ." '

As always, the roguish 'comic look' was the one he turned towards me. God was 'G-d' or 'You Know Who'. In a letter (13 July 1979) inviting Bob and me to Woodroyd:

> Long to see you both, & this is a particularly good time because G-d has invited himself for just those days. You know how we've been longing for you & Bob to meet him; and vice versa, I may say, with knobs on. We just *know* you'll simply love each other – all three. He has so much more sheer charm than they tend to say.

In another letter:

> Do come here as soon as possible. Lots to talk about. For instance I've got a completely new line on G-d, which you'll love.

Another:

> Am now trying to write a book about G-d, but he doesn't seem
> to be giving much cooperation. Perhaps it's because I want to
> say that he is'nt *nearly* so powerful as most suppose. What's
> *your* next ploy?

June 1977:

> I'm trying to write a book about G-d so persuasive that even
> you will suddenly find yourself down on your hunkers staring
> up at the sky . . .

I made an effort to answer in kind:

> We'd love to come to Woodroyd. Will G-d really be coming, &
> if so will He mind sharing the David Astor bathroom? I only
> ask because from what I've read about Him in the Old Testa-
> ment & His other Public Relations handouts He doesn't sound
> like the sharing type. In fact He often gets a bit *jealous* (see, e.g.,
> Exodus XX 4).

Friends Apart, long out of print, was reissued in 1980 by
Sidgwick and Jackson, with a new introduction by Philip in
which he discussed his 'radically changed . . . attitude to the
nature of man and his life on earth':

> Having become a sort of Christian, and certainly a believer in
> the Christian God of Love, the transcendent realm of Heaven, I
> wonder, now, whether the deaths of my friends were really so
> absolute an end, for them and us, as they seemed to be at the
> time. Are those young men still in some sense *there*, after all, in
> whatever inconceivably altered state of being and conscious-
> ness?

Knowing that Philip would expect a comment from me on
this strangely-imagined circumstance, I wrote:

Imagine Esmond in the 'transcendent realm of Heaven'! It would jolly well have to be an 'inconceivably altered state of being & consciousness,' as you say. I can't imagine him getting on with all those angels. Teaching Gabriel to play Carmagnole on his horn? Getting after St Peter re his restrictive admissions policy? Starting up a new edition of Out of Bounds? That would get him nowhere but DOWN, don't you agree?

In his *Radio Times* profile, Philip wrote of me:

The weapon she adopts in most of her muckraking books and articles is precisely that sharp clownish ridicule with which she regards such enterprises as our Gloucestershire commune and such attitudes as my own growing concern with religious belief and Christian practice. When I read *The American Way of Death* . . . there were even moments when I felt a touch of sympathy for those disgraceful 'morticians' as they came under a lash which I have sometimes felt curl – though lightly, for an old friend – around my own shoulders.

This mock-defensive posture perhaps explains the special tone of his letters to me, so different from that of his serious writing and letters to others.

For example, in May 1978 he suffered the horrible blow of the death of Ben Nicolson, his best friend for three decades. In *Part of a Journey* he writes:

Darkness falls from the air . . . Coldness as well as darkness. Wild, uncontrollable sobbing as I tried to make sense of what Pinkie had told me . . . The dear, long, clerical face, and the solemn voice which I knew so well that I perfected my imitation of more than thirty years ago . . . What will they make of him at Heaven's Gate; or he of them? Ben, for whom any notion of the spirit was not just alien but totally incomprehensible; never for a moment attracting even his hostile attention.

But to me he wrote:

Ben's loss is frightful: Sally & I reminding ourselves of marvellous Bennish episodes of the past. The Times obit said 'innocent but wily', which is dead right. He never washed a single dish on at least 100 visits to Anne & me, then Sally & me; always managed to be suddenly extra vague just when the work started.

The fist-shaking persisted (August 1980):

Will send *Part of a Journey* as soon as I have a decent copy. You won't like it much – well, you may like some bits, but not the parts about You Know Who. (What's so rotten is that He's not going to like it either.)

The last letter I had on this subject (9 January 1981):

Actually I tend to believe, from latest evidence, that we *all* get excellent treatment from the very moment of dropping off the hooks. I certainly feel we all deserve it, seeing how tough things have been over here, one way or another. (Well, perhaps H. Himmler might have to do three or four minutes in Purgatory; but I'm sure he'd see the point as soon as it was put to him by those simply angelic guides) . . . I continue to march steadily backwards in my search for You Know Who. But I understand this is the usual form, and far from discouraging.

While Philip's friends and contemporaries made a stab at comprehending the mystery of his conversion, it was Jason who perhaps came closest to getting it in focus.

I see what happened to his ideas in the last twelve or so years of his life, very crudely as follows. He realized that ideas about how life should be led (politics, socialism, morality) are empty unless put into action in one's own, everyday life – the 'alternative'. He tried to do this by setting up a community, but found that he couldn't handle practical collectivism, and that the family hated this environment.

Simultaneously he turned to God as the source of love. No materialist explanation seemed adequate for saintliness or ordinary goodness, and he was fascinated by the huge corpus of religious experience, which could not be dismissed without arrogance or prejudice. After he left the Community he adopted the position that 'one cannot live beyond one's moral means' to support his return to a conventional (though more frugal) lifestyle. He concentrated more and more on the idea of the Holy Spirit and the ways it is revealed to people: all loving, but by no means omnipotent, its full strength glimpsed and felt rarely, but falling diffused and patchily on to humanity.

I find this very convincing, although I don't share his 'faith'. Far from having gone soft, or become sentimental, I think my father became an unapologetic believer in God through intellectual firmness.

Part of a Journey came out in the spring of 1981, a few months before Philip died. He was right: I *didn't* much like the parts about You Know Who, although I cherish the nuggets of autobiography, rare glimpses of his enduring, still passionate love for Sally and fond feelings for his children.

I think that Jason's point – that Philip became 'an unapologetic believer in God through intellectual firmness' – is borne out in his book. For a serious appraisal of *Part of a Journey*, unencumbered by my own encrusted prejudices, I quote from a review by Marina Warner in *The Sunday Times* entitled 'St Toynbee'. Philip must have rejoiced in this evaluation by a young and brilliant writer, a contemporary of his own daughters; there is nothing so satisfying as finding favour with a younger generation.

> Sainthood hasn't been a respectable ambition in intellectual circles – 'enlightened circles' – for a long time [wrote Marina Warner]. It's one which, if admitted at all, leads friends to wince and shuffle their feet, and acquaintances further afield to jeer.

Wincing, shuffling and jeering I read on:

Even Camus's question – how to be a saint without God – has a dangerously pious air about it. Philip Toynbee in *Part of a Journey* never tells us in so many words that he wants to be a saint; even his robust and unequivocal avowal of belief fights shy of making such an admission, and he is too entertaining and penetrating a writer to stifle us with sermons.

It's wildly improbable, preposterous even, that any man of letters, with Arnold Toynbee for a father, Gilbert Murray for a grandfather and a whole backdrop of Babylonian stews and their worldly wisdom and scepticism and dandyism could ever invite comparison with . . . The Little Flower, Saint Thérèse. But there is a fellowship – though Toynbee is never cloying and mawkish . . .

She concludes:

It takes a true, passionate renegade from conventions to remind us how eloquent and rich the search can be, even if his commitment can only be observed, not shared.

For a side of Philip seldom shown to me – or for that matter, to others of his earlier acquaintance – I must turn to his late-blooming correspondence from 1977 to 1981 with Ann Farrer, widow of the actor David Horne.

As background: Unknown to me (for I was in America at the time), Ann suffered the almost unimaginable torture of a severe nervous breakdown. Later, she wrote a book about the experience: *If Hopes Were Dupes*, published in July 1966. My sisters and I thought it the best book on this dire subject we had ever read. I was confident that it would be embraced by a large general readership for its intrinsic excellence, and by fellow-sufferers for the light it shed on a shared malady.

These expectations did not materialize. Nancy, who thought very highly of *If Hopes Were Dupes*, faulted the title as too obscure. (It comes from a poem by Arthur Hugh Clough: 'If hopes were dupes, fears may be liars.' Andrew Devonshire misheard this line as: 'If hopes were dukes, peers may be liars.')

She thought a title more directly describing the subject would have made for better sales.

I happened to be in London a few months after Ann's book was published. To my extreme disappointment, it seemed to have sunk without a trace.

Longing to revive it, I sent a copy to Philip, asking if he could review it in *The Observer*. As I had hoped, it struck an instant responsive chord; he liked it enormously, but explained that it was against *The Observer* policy to give a full-scale review to a book that had been out for some time. He would try to sneak in something under 'Shorter Notices'.

He wrote to Ann (28 October 1966): 'I thought it extremely well done – dreadfully vivid . . . Decca tells me I was once sick on your floor. Quite enough to start anybody off on a neurosis! With best wishes, Philip.' The Shorter Notice (*The Observer*, 1 December 1966) heaped praise: 'She emerged from the darkness at last. Her courageous return to those appalling shadows will be read with great benefit by all lonely sufferers from mental and nervous affliction.'

Six years after David Horne's death in 1970, Ann went to live in Old Jordans, a Quaker hostel in Buckinghamshire. Still suffering from bouts of depression, she also fell prey to a progressively painful physical condition. She tried to find solace in writing poetry, selections from which she sent to me. I forwarded them to Philip, reminding him of his admiration of her book.

He immediately wrote to Ann, and a pen-pal relationship soon developed in which they exchanged letters almost weekly. Eventually he and Sally went to see her in the Quaker hostel. He reported to me (26 August 1978):

> The good news is that we went to visit Ann Horne & simply loved her. So reminiscent of you in so many ways; we do hope she will become a close friend in spite of her difficulty in moving. What a life she's had, poor thing. But such good

company, and full of such wise & discriminating admiration
for the writings of P. Toynbee.

A few months later (15 January 1979):

> Our relations with Ann are very close, and very precious to us.
> Letters rush to & fro, and we plan to visit her again in that
> extraordinary sort of rich man's workhouse as soon as the
> weather gets bearable.

Their correspondence dwelt on Ann's poetry, to which
Philip gave serious critical attention; the depressions to which
both were subject; and a shared belief in a spiritual life.

His letters about her poems, a marvellous mixture of praise
for those he thought successful and careful criticism on an
almost line-for-line basis when he thought she had gone off the
track, could serve as a primer from which any writer could
profit:

> [12 May 1979]:
>
> Now as for *Untitled*, I really do think this is the best you have
> sent me so far: it feels as if it sprang straight out of your
> anguish, like a ghastly birth. But also a beautiful birth. I truly
> think it very good . . .
>
> Only one criticism – 'music a mockery.' This is the kind of
> neat phrase which seems marvellous at first, but I don't think it
> will stand up for long . . . Of course I can't suggest anything;
> but when music means nothing to me, as all too often, I feel it's
> an empty exercise in brilliance: – 'Oh well done! Jolly good!
> But please, please, please stop showing off.' Finally it just
> becomes thump-thump; tinkle-tinkle; boom-boom-boom
> . . . It *is* a mockery, yes, but I don't think the word really does
> the trick.

> [22 June 1979]:
>
> *Double Entry* rang so many sad bells for me: worse than sad;
> bells tolling our utter desolation in which nothing but fear

stays alive. Really, you know, there is no bond so close as a
shared hell. I always feel that you are in a rather deeper, and
therefore more distinguished, part of it than I am. But I do
know what it feels like down there – and love you very much
for describing it so well.

[1974 or 1975:]

You ought, like almost all of us, to concentrate on the concrete
& the specific; leave the big emotions, statements etc. to make
themselves felt through 'discarded pencils by the splint &
bandages.'

Everything comes to life here: the objects are more than
symbols; they are sacramental; sacraments of pain, to put it
rather heavily.

I think you are a natural observer of such minutiae, which I,
alas, am not. It is a great gift; and I feel sure that if you learn
how to use it even more richly you will write really well.

I do hope this has been some help. Wish I could be more.
Anyway please accept a wave of the hand from a fellow-
sufferer at present deep in the trough of a particularly virulent
depression.

His cautions against the use of hackneyed phrases are (to use
a hackneyed phrase) gems of literary criticism.

[12 June 1978:]

I think your pieces on music are a bit too grandiloquent: and I
don't think, for example, that 'depths' can be 'plumbed' any
longer. The strange thing about language is that marvellous
phrases simply get used up and refuse to do any more work.
Yet the danger is that if one carefully avoids them this often
shows in the form of something outlandish and self-conscious.
I suppose you simply have to wait and *feel* for the real, right,
true words. Or else try and try and try again, until suddenly
something true and good stumbles out of the mess . . .

I think the second [poem] better than the first – but even then
–'highest calls to highest'! I know exactly what you mean, but
the words themselves are dead, for me, because of too many
uneasy associations.

I wish I could say something cheerier; but I'd be no use to you unless I said what I really think.

[19 August 1975:]

There is a tendency to over-familiar language – 'naked depths' 'heart-breaking', 'heroic resignation', 'courage born of despair.' The difficulty is that phrases like these are lodged firmly in all our minds, and when we consciously try to get rid of them we tend to fall into the opposite fault of using outlandish and unnatural language.

[21 November:]

I now notice something which I don't think will quite do – namely 'desperate moments of despair.' This is what I believe they call a tautology. Seems to me that if you simply leave out 'desperate' it sounds better altogether. No?

[2 January 1978:]

About your dream – I don't think you should worry too much about finding the right words to describe it. I suspect that we are most of us much too preoccupied with words; almost slaves to them. We don't feel that anything is quite real until we've found the best possible words to describe it. Yet the 'best possible words' may really be a betrayal of the experience, because we have probably chosen those words as the ones most likely to impress an imaginary reader. Who's talking, you may well exclaim. But when I look back on much of my own writing life I realize that I have indeed been writing to impress rather than writing to tell the truth.

[29 December 1979:]

Now, I draw my breath, daring myself to reveal the terrible extent of my fatuity. Wd you believe that when I first read this splendid piece I thought it might be about ME: and was quite cross when I found you were addressing Ludwig von Berthoffen or whatever his name is. I tell you this so that you will never underestimate my egomania – a sort of jack-in-the-box which I can usually keep down but who springs out and gives a great squawk at the lightest touch on his catch.

Occasionally, Ann was wounded by Philip's failure to comment on a poem she had sent, taking this to mean that he had not liked it – which no doubt was sometimes the case. His reply sets forth his views of the creative process.

[12 August 1980:]

Believe me, dear Ann, I know those kind of feelings and have often experienced them in the past . . .

In fact I have never written anything which was so much a projection of my inmost self that I regarded an attack on it as an attack on me. Nor do I believe that the process of creation is of this kind: there is always a necessary and *inevitable* distancing of the writer, painter etc from his work. The idea of pouring out one's heart straight onto the paper is, I believe, a romantic illusion; and rather a dangerous one . . .

In the course of writing *Pantaloon* I had just such feelings of absolute rightness, glorious confidence, only to discover later that these feelings had utterly misled me. Sometimes I wrote for as much as six months as if inspired; then found that I had to scrap almost every word of what I had done and start all over again. This is one of the very hard facts about trying to write: nearly always it is a matter of hard slogging and constant revision, rather than the Muse suddenly touching one's shoulder or receiving one's words direct from heaven.

[15 October 1980:]

I think that when one writes burningly out of one's own experience, still filled with the overflowing emotions of real life, one usually misses one's aim. Who wrote about 'emotion recollected in tranquillity'? Anyway, I'm sure that in nearly all cases there has to be a real pause, a taking stock, however unconscious, a distancing . . . Then the emotions are still there all right, but they are just far enough away for one to be able to marshall them; order them about; then alter the whole emphasis of them for the sake of the poem. After all, a poem is always an artifact; indeed an artifice. Put another way, if the bleeding wounds still show then I think there is something wrong. (Except in very very rare cases).

On the other hand I *loved* 'The Angels Look Down'; and I think the first verse is the best bit of writing you've ever sent me. Here you manage to write out of your own experience, but also to generalize it so that it is shared by us all. Yet you also keep it particular in detail of expression. In fact, jolly well done, old girl. Absolutely super! I mean it.

At the time he was corresponding with Ann, Philip was writing *Part of a Journey*. Perhaps, discerning in Ann a fellow-believer, he may have used her as a sounding board for material he intended to incorporate into his book. In my view his letters to her are more direct, and reveal more candidly his innermost thoughts than anything that eventually emerged in print:

[23 September:]

So far as the spirit goes I am almost like a tone-deaf person trying to listen to music. The *will* is there; immense eagerness; readiness to devote most of my life (it should be all) to the endless journey. And I do hear faint whispers of joy from time to time; perhaps see the tip of an angel's wing as he (she?) scoots away at my approach . . . But none of this bothers me very much, since I now know that we simply have to do the best we can with the equipment we've got, & not fuss at all about how far *on* we are . . .

All my life I've been trying over & over again to live beyond my moral means. Starting on some grand course of self-sacrifice, virtue etc, then falling flat on my face in the mud. Of course we should aim high and all that, but aiming too high is just another form of foolish vanity. And gets its deserts accordingly.

[25 October 1978:]

Somehow all my faults seem to have been oozing out of me with particular virulence in the last few days – weeks, perhaps. Self, self, SELF! Greed; anger; impatience; fear. My prayers seem even emptier than usual, & my use to others almost non-existent. (I know you sweetly write that I've been some use to you, but at times like these I feel that this whole thing has been nothing but an act, me pretending to be a sweet, kindly, concerned friend when all I really want is to be told what a sweet, kindly, concerned friend I am. Ugh!)

[3 November 1978:]

Many, many thanks for all the prayers & love winging out of Old Jordans & all the way to Glos. They speeded up my recovery a great deal, and I am now my usual fairly hearty self. (Do you find that prayer is almost impossible either if one's too high or too low? I have to catch those days of unusual sensibility when joy & sadness seem to be mixed inextricably together.)

[9 December 1978:]

I seem to believe more & more each time I write about Christianity, but without a single jot of personal experience to give me grounds. Very strange. Anyway I still *just* hope for a direct message from above one of these days; or rather nights. Do you too?

[27 February 1980:]

At the moment I'm trying to write a piece about EVIL – I don't mean PAIN, but real wickedness. The more I think about it the more it seems to evaporate; but I have begun to get a few ideas down. The chief one is that, contrary to what Christianity has always supposed, the basic cause of all our woe and evil is not pride but FEAR.

[26 November 1977:]

I have taken to looking at trees – really looking, for the first time in my life. A strong sense of actuality; not the joyful communion with nature which so many have felt and written about, but a feeling of very strong reality, as if, could I look even harder and better, I would see the tree in that higher reality which I know *about* but have seldom if ever known.

In general I think the most positive effect of my prayers and meditations – perhaps of my depression too – has been to slow me up in a most glorious way. I've been rushing through life until now, constantly in a state of wild impatience, always wanting most urgently to get to the next place. Now I try to do everything with deliberation, attention and respect: often fail, of course, but feel very happy when I succeed.

I love your letters: thank you so much for them. We seem to communicate very naturally, and I'm sure the spirit is with us.

Needless to say, while I was in intermittent correspondence with both at the time, Philip and Ann had wisely written me off as a lost cause in their quest for loftier realms and heavenly intervention through prayer. Ann to Philip (18 February 1981):

> Decca wrote saying that she was praying for what she calls Debo's 'Adept' [a back specialist recommended by my sister] but said she didn't think it would do much good as she hasn't prayed since she was 5, when it went like this: 'God bless mother and father, brother and sisters and Nanny, and make Decca a good girl. Amen.' She added, 'He didn't do *any* of that.'

In *Part of a Journey*, Philip describes his latent depression:

> It seems like an animal lying curled-up inside me – on the left hand side. Most of the time he's asleep, but sometimes he shudders and stirs in his sleep; sometimes he quakes all over, the fur rising on his back; sometimes he even opens his mouth wide in a huge snarling yawn.

He wrote to Ann about these horrors:

> [19 August 1975:]
> I have been much better lately – though I still feel as if I were walking on a spider's web which could break and let me fall

through again at any moment. I feel sure that I *have* learnt something from two years of intermittent agony, though it is hard indeed to find the right words for it . . .

Meanwhile, all my love and sympathy, and the strong hope that you too are beginning to emerge from the hell we both know all too well.

[23 September 1978:]

Your splendid communications always do me a tremendous amount of good – or do I mean harm. Well, good in that they are so full of love and goodwill; harm in that my ego immediately begins to swell almost to bursting as I read your words of admiration. Still, on the whole I think most of us need a bit of boosting, don't you, and are quite capable of deflating the balloon with a sharp reminiscent prick or two as soon as it starts to look too ridiculous.

One thing that Sally & I both feel very strongly, which is that you are a tremendous under-self-estimator. So please accept a few sharp strokes of the bicycle pump – e.g., that you are a most lovable, humble, amusing, intelligent & individual person; that we both hope you will be our ever-dearer friend for life; that we loved being with you & pass each page of your letters eagerly from hand to hand. Particular admiration and amazement at your private discovery of music and prolonged voyage of discovery ever since.

[30 June 1979:]

We *loved* your visit . . . Your letter gave us the greatest possible pleasure. It is often hard for us to believe that we give an impression of peace, calm, love etc., since we are all too often in a state of distraction & misery. But I do believe that what you felt about us is true, however often obscured, and that in the end the obscurities will fade away. Oh *God*, for that day! When we have the peace of God between us and within us, so that we can give it to others.

[21 July 1979:]

Just back from two fearsome, though sober, days in London. Much though I love seeing old friends & dear family, the whole place fills me with horror & fear. All so changed & strange: I took two buses going the wrong way, & had to suffer a long tube journey in the rush-hour. How those poor people can avoid going raving mad I shall never understand.

Anyway I succeeded, after hours of nightmare search, in finding and buying a computerized chess-challenger – which is proving even more fun than we'd hoped. We also have two tremendous new bicycles, but have'nt yet dared to mount them . . .

My feeling is that a brilliant angel does indeed bring certain passages (of poems); then hands over to some rather pathetic & incompetent colleague to help with the rest. Or – more seriously – that God can sometimes reach us directly and easily, but usually only when we are working like anything to do the thing ourselves.

[23 October 1979:]

Am rather prostrated, alas, with post-guest depression – so *please* forgive a very inadequate answer to your last.

Clued in by Sally, whom I always rang up first thing on arrival in London, I began to realize that all contact with people except for herself and his children was becoming increasingly painful to Philip; and I worried about his massive correspondence with Ann, feeling rather guilty for having initiated it in the first place. I must have cautioned her against overwhelming him with letters, for he wrote to her (12 December 1979):

No, Decca is quite wrong in thinking that your letters are any sort of strain . . . I would be *appalled* if you stopped writing.

Letters, then, were evidently not unwelcome; Sally tells me that he kept up a huge correspondence with all sorts of people, including several unpublished poets who sent him their work for his ever-generous criticism.

Visitors were another matter. In *Part of a Journey* Philip describes a 'post-guest depression' of December 1977:

> Having Paddy and Joan for the weekend was an insanely heroic enterprise; and all the time I was painfully acting the part of the boon companion I used to be in their infinitely exhilarating company. (Paddy and I – perfect foils for each other's clownish extravagances.) The strain was almost unremitting; and I saw these dear old friends drive away at last with a sense of melting relief: retreated instantly to bed and a day's collapse.

Once in a while – but more and more infrequently – the depression would lift. In September 1979 he and Sally came for a weekend to the Jenkins's house near Rye, where Bob and I were also staying. Philip was very much his old self; he threw himself into the pleasures of family life, organized elaborate games, races, treasure-hunts for his wide-eyed little grandchildren who were clearly fascinated by his antics.

He described the weekend in *Part of a Journey*: 'A very cheerful visit . . . Decca and I clowned away as of yore . . . pleasant games with the children.' On the way down he and Sally had called on Ann: 'As usual this was a happy and very talkative meeting, with much more to say than we had time for.'

They had a

> vigorous discussion on reincarnation . . . When I talked about this to Decca, she told a very funny story: Wife, in touch with dead husband through medium: 'Well, dear, what do you do over there?' 'Oh, we run about a bit; then we eat a bit; then we have a bit of sex; then we run about a bit again; have a bit more to eat, and a bit more sex . . . ' Wife: 'Goodness, I never knew heaven was like that.' Husband: 'Oh I'm not in heaven. I'm a rabbit in Australia.'

Later that month the Toynbees were planning a walking tour, a pilgrimage in which they would visit various French shrines, from Mont St Michel to Chartres Cathedral. Bob and I were to be in France at the same time, with a hired car; emboldened by Philip's sociable mood at the Jenkins's, I suggested meeting up in Chartres for a bit of conviviality. And so it was arranged. As they would be hoofing it for hundreds of miles through the French countryside, with no way of getting in touch, we agreed to meet at the west front of the cathedral at 11 a.m. on 21 September.

Fearing to be late, Bob and I arrived in Chartres on the evening before. We wandered out to dinner in a restaurant next to our hotel – and there were the Toynbees, having got there before us like the Clever Little Pig outwitting the wolf. I cross-examined Philip about the walking tour – had they really come on foot all the way from the coast? He reluctantly admitted that for the most part they had hiked in and out of bus depots and train stations.

> When we described our journey Decca promptly calculated that we'd carried our packs for an average of only 1.4 miles a day [he wrote in *Part of a Journey*]. 'Ah,' I said, 'but you must remember all those hard slogs from the station to the station hotel.' But I must admit that her teasing calculation did rather put the 'pilgrimage' in its place.
>
> One might cast B and D – a last fling of that now forbidden fantasy – as the appointed Mockers: not hostile, in my mythology, to the Vièrge du Pilier, but charged by her to lighten the solemnity of her adorers.

This was also our last fling with Philip. I never saw him again. In the two years before his death Sally wisely and devotedly kept most visitors at bay; he could no longer tolerate the strain of entertaining old friends – least of all, I imagine, 'appointed Mockers'. Yet in his new social milieu, the Anglican convent in Tymawr where he spent much time, he was himself a bit of a mocker. Joan A. M. Davis, a lay member of the convent wrote to me (1 September 1983) describing his behaviour as an aspirant nun:

> On Sundays after Mass and breakfast Philip and Sister Paula and other nuns would repair to the library. Philip would then try to startle them by some heretical outrageous proposition and Sister Paula would point out his theological errors. He teased her and she him. He became – with some misgivings – an associate member of their society, and I think he felt honoured and proud of their love and their confidence in him. The hours he spent with the nuns and in their chapel were perhaps the most tranquil and happy of his life.

Philip's writings, with their enormous range from his delightful, highly readable articles and reviews to the extremely complex *Pantaloon* series, will be his ultimate monument. For those of us who knew him, the picture that stays with us is a more personal – typically Philip – one.

The obituary notices of his friends afford a composite drawing like those police sketches of a wanted person, from which emerges the many-sidedness of this curious character and the underlying (sometimes concealed) sweetness of his nature.

Robert Kee:

> *Observer* readers who will have appreciated over many years his searching honesty of mind may not always have been able to perceive through the distance of the printed page the abounding energy of his sense of fun. It was his great gift to be able to infuse this sense of fun into his most serious and often painful thoughts, so that for all his personal and intellectual restlessness he was able to achieve, with the loving help of his wife and family, in spite of grim bouts of depression, a sort of equilibrium, if any word so dull-sounding can be used to express his charming and indignant sanity of mind.

Noel Annan:

He was marked with the brand of the Thirties, a sense of hopelessness that the evils of the world flourished and nothing would uproot them, and a sense of how ludicrous the ways of the world were, but the ludicrous included himself. Temperamentally he liked to go too far. Then he would contemplate the results wryly, ruefully, and sometimes sadly . . .

Through his reviews spoke the voice of someone who was both honest and honourable, deprecating about his own beliefs which he advanced with modesty, nearly always respectful of those with which he disagreed. He never stamped upon his past.

He never stamped on anyone. He genuinely hated the lacerating, snide, malicious, personalized style of reviewing posing as righteous discrimination.

Peter Vansittart:

A certain boyishness long remained with his sudden crazes – for a garden game, a tape recorder, the ten-gear bicycle which I suspect he never really used; for dire home-made wines which briefly impaired his reputation for hospitality.

Part of a Journey contains austere inner wrestling, tortured set-backs, rueful intimations of absurdity, brave strivings for cohesion, acceptance grace . . .

'December 9th. I have resolved to give up booze entirely.'

'December 10th. An exception will be made, of course, on Christmas day.'

Robert Nye:

When I first met Philip Toynbee he launched into an attack on the dogma of the Trinity which turned quickly into an even more impassioned analysis of the mystery of why three stumps go to make up a wicket in cricket. He carried a flagon of home-brewed ale under his arm, smoked hand-rolled cigarettes like a man sucking food down a tube, and took out his false teeth every now and again to illustrate a point.

David Astor:

Philip's love of people and loyalty to them was one of his most striking characteristics. Whether in an exalted mood or a low one, you could count on him never to falter in a relationship. Apart from his great capacity for friendship, he brought a wonderful equality of feeling for literally everyone. There was no one in the office whom he ignored: and there was no visitor to our Observer lunches, no matter how eminent or awe-inspiring, whom he did not treat quite naturally as a brother, when the rest of us might be treating the great man either with awe or disdain. Not Philip: he levelled everyone up and talked with a freedom that he could get away with because he was as deeply good-hearted as he was intelligent.

A. J. Ayer:

Philip reminded me in many ways of James Boswell, in his zest for experience, his lack of worldly caution, his physical indulgence, his ease in making friends, his addiction to journalizing, his profound changes of mood. I dare say even that the absence of a Dr Johnson contributed to his looking to religion for security . . . He strove hard to attain his religious belief and it brought him to the point where he was not afraid of death.

The last observation is borne out in a letter to Ann Farrer written many months before his final illness:

[2 February 1980:]

I've been reading a lot of Life after Death books, & am slowly but enthusiastically coming round to the view that we *do* get a second chance – *not* on this rotten old earth! – and very likely a third and a fourth ad infinitum until we become *both* joyful and angelically good. Seems a long way off from this end, though.

Am now busily continuing the journal [*Part of a Journey*] and can't really see how it will ever end. Until I do. In fact from what I now read I may be carrying on with it OVER THERE, so long as the harps don't disturb too much.

A few months later he wrote to me, tongue as always firmly in cheek:

> Trouble is we live such hermit-lives that we never have any news for old friends. However the hills seem to get a little bit lower & and the valleys not quite so deep – so perhaps our last years will be a glorious glide through the air in a holy haze.

Index

A NOTE ON THE TYPE

The text of this book was set in a digitized version of Bembo, the well-known Monotype face. Named for Pietro Bembo, the celebrated Renaissance writer and humanist scholar who was made a cardinal and served as secretary to Pope Leo X, the original cutting of Bembo was made by Francesco Griffo of Bologna only a few years after Columbus discovered America.

Sturdy, well balanced, and finely proportioned, Bembo is a face of rare beauty and extremely legible in all of its sizes.

Printed and bound by
The Haddon Craftsmen, Inc.,
Scranton, Pennsylvania